OECD Handbook on Measuring the Space Economy

OECD

This work is published on the responsibility of the Secretary-General of the OECD. The opinions expressed and arguments employed herein do not necessarily reflect the official views of the Organisation or of the governments of its member countries.

This document and any map included herein are without prejudice to the status of or sovereignty over any territory, to the delimitation of international frontiers and boundaries and to the name of any territory, city or area.

Please cite this publication as:
OECD (2012), *OECD Handbook on Measuring the Space Economy*, OECD Publishing.
http://dx.doi.org/10.1787/9789264169166-en

ISBN 978-92-64-12180-5 (print)
ISBN 978-92-64-16916-6 (PDF)

Photo credits: Cover © Stocktrek/Corbis.

Corrigenda to OECD publications may be found on line at: *www.oecd.org/publishing/corrigenda*.

Foreword

The Handbook to Measuring the Space Economy *is the result of collective efforts within the framework of the OECD International Futures Programme (IFP), aimed at better understanding the space sector and its wider economic dimensions.*

The work is part of a systematic effort within the OECD to understand and assess the potential economic, social and environmental benefits of new economic sectors, based on technological innovations that contribute to productivity gains in the economy and society at large. Information and communication technologies (ICT), biotechnology-based applications, and space-based applications are parts of this group of actual or potential drivers.

As the space economy develops, policy-makers, investors, members of the public and private sector and academia increasingly call for access to comparable statistical data from major space faring nations and their space industry. As the Handbook *suggests this requires more work and co-operation internationally. Although useful indicators and statistics already exist, a number of methodological obstacles still remain in order to more accurately quantify the space sector and render data comparable across countries.*

Contributing to the emergence of economic data, the Forum on Space Economics – the OECD Space Forum – was launched to investigate the economic dimensions and implications of the space infrastructure for the larger economy. This innovative platform includes a number of governments and space agencies as founders: ASI (Agenzia Spaziale Italiana, the Italian Space Agency), CNES (Centre National d'Etudes Spatiales, the French Space Agency), CSA (Canadian Space Agency), ESA (European Space Agency), NASA (National Aeronautics and Space Administration), NOAA (National Oceanic and Atmospheric Administration), Norwegian Space Centre (Norsk Romsenter), the UK Space Agency and USGS (United States Geological Survey). Other actors in governmental agencies, the space industry, academia, industry associations, and consulting firms are regularly involved in the Forum activities. The Space Economy at A Glance *(2007, 2011) is one of several outputs of the Forum. It paints a detailed picture of the space industry, its downstream services activities, and its wider economic and social impacts. In parallel, case studies are conducted in the Forum to explore the specific economic impacts of space applications in various sectors. Two publications summarise the findings so far* Space Technologies and Climate Change *(2008) and* Space Technologies and Food Security *(2012, forthcoming).*

The Handbook to Measuring the Space Economy *builds on the OECD Space Forum's analytical groundwork and provides a comprehensive approach to measuring the space economy. It takes stock of current issues surrounding measurements of the space economy's contours, identifies the main obstacles to be overcome, and presents several avenues for improvements in economic data. More work is needed to better map statistically the space sector and its downstream activities, and ongoing international co-operation is key to address a number of challenges identified in this publication.*

The report was prepared by Claire Jolly, OECD Policy Analyst, under the direction and guidance of Barrie Stevens, Head of the International Futures Programme and Pierre-Alain Schieb, Head of Futures Projects. Anita Gibson provided administrative and editorial assistance. The team has benefited from many contributions since the beginning of the Forum, including suggestions from Colin Webb, Directorate for Science, Technology and Industry (DSTI) and the initial support of Paul Schreyer and Andreas Lindner of the Statistics Directorate. Thanks also go to Dirk Pilat and Sandrine Kergroach-Connan of DSTI whose 2002 paper commissioned by the IFP was the building block in the development of this work. Experts from other organisations also contributed useful inputs, including A. Malfara, Senior Classifications Specialist from Statistics Canada. Our thanks go to members of the OECD Space Forum, who contributed expertise, ideas and data. Our thanks go also to experts in the space community from industry associations, consulting firms and academia, particularly to Pierre Lionnet from Eurospace, Norihiro Sakamoto formerly from the Society of Japanese Aerospace Companies and Henry Hertzfeld from the Space Policy Institute.

Table of Contents

Part I

Basics on Measuring the Space Economy

Part II

Overview of Indicators for the Space Economy

Tables

Figures

PART I

Basics on Measuring the Space Economy

PART I

Chapter 1

Introduction

The introduction provides answers to the following questions: Why has the Handbook *been produced? Who is the intended audience for the* Handbook*? What does the* Handbook *contain?*

The *Handbook* and its rationale

The *Handbook to Measuring the Space Economy* is part of a broader systematic effort within the OECD to understand and assess the contribution of new sectors to economic and social development more generally.

This involves looking beyond the core sector to explore its wider interactions with other sectors and other markets. Thus, in the past, attention has shifted for example from the ICT sector to the information economy, from the biotechnology sector to the bio economy, and more recently from the space sector to the space economy (OECD, 2011a).

Like the information economy and the bio economy, the concept of the space economy endeavours to capture the numerous complex value chains and downstream applications that reach into many aspects of economic and social life. Moreover, in the current economic context, the search is on to identify new potential sources of economic growth. The space economy, with its vast array of scientific, technical, environmental, business and consumer applications is a particularly promising field of study. For all the aforementioned reasons, it is crucial to improve our ability to measure the space economy.

Work on space activities at OECD

As part of its mission, the OECD IFP is examining how space technologies could potentially affect the general economy.

- A two-year in-depth project (2002-04) on the potential of space applications conducted in collaboration with private and public actors from the international space community resulted in two publications: *Space 2030: The Future of Space Applications* (OECD, 2004) explored promising space applications for the 21st century. *Space 2030: Tackling Society's Challenges* (OECD, 2005) assessed the strengths and weaknesses of the regulatory frameworks that govern space and formulated a policy framework that OECD governments might use in drafting policies to ensure that the potential offered by space is fully realised. Following this project, there was a demand for the OECD to lead further innovative economic analysis of the sector and to create a dedicated Forum, complementing other existing institutional structures.

- The OECD Space Forum's mission is to investigate the economic dimensions and implications of space infrastructure for the wider economy. It published *The Space Economy at a Glance*, the first OECD statistical overview of the emerging space economy, a novel compilation of statistics on the space sector and its contributions to economic activity (OECD, 2007). An updated version was released in the summer of 2011 (OECD, 2011b). In parallel to statistical activities, case studies on space applications are conducted to examine the socio-economic impacts of space applications in diverse sectors. As a first step, this work has resulted in the publication of *Space Technologies and Climate Change (OECD, 2008)*. Focussing on examples of water management, marine resources and maritime transport, the report critically looks at the arguments for developing satellite systems that measure and monitor climate change and help mitigate its consequences. A second forthcoming publication examines the contributions of space applications in global food supplies (*i.e.* agriculture and fisheries production, transport, distribution networks).

Users of the *Handbook*

As in the case of other manuals published by the OECD, the audience of this *Handbook* includes a broad range of users.

- policy makers and representatives of governmental agencies form a major part of the demand for more detailed information on the space sector;
- commercial actors, active in the space community and beyond, many of whom have contributed data and analysis for this *Handbook*, as well as potential investors in space products and services;
- researchers in different disciplines and policy or financial analysts who interpret statistical information and need to access the methodologies that underlie that information;
- and finally, international organisations, whose information requirements centre on comparability across countries, are part of the target audience.

Scope and content

This *Handbook* is intended to assist in the consistent application of concepts and definitions, as well as the collection of comparable data via statistical surveys.

- the report identifies the obstacles to reliable measurement of key aspects of the space economy and offers several avenues for data improvements;
- It complements the publication *The Space Economy at a Glance 2011*, while also providing a compendium of indicators that are currently available, with methodological notes for users.

The methodologies and indicators on the space economy are presented here in a framework that consists of three interdependent categories: readiness (inputs), intensity (outputs), and impacts:

- The readiness factors of the space economy, which include the different elements that are necessary for the development of space activities. These elements encompass the technical, financial and social infrastructures that enable the production of space-related hardware or the provision of services, *i.e.* government budgets for space activities (both for public space programmes and for R&D activities) and human capital.
- The intensity indicators of the space economy; which are constituted by all the diverse outputs (products, services, science) that are produced or provided by the space sector. These outputs are very diverse in nature, from commercial revenues from industry, scientific outputs such as patents, to number of satellites, space missions or space launches.
- The impacts indicators of the space economy, which include various types of socio-economic impacts derived from the development of space activities. Four main categories of impacts have been identified so far, although further work is certainly needed on the social dimensions of the use of space applications (*e.g.* reduction of the digital divide via satellite communications); they include: the creation of new commercial products and services, productivity/efficiency gains in diverse economic sectors (*e.g.* fisheries, airlines), economic growth regionally and nationally, and cost avoidances (*e.g.* floods).

The diagram below illustrates the different steps from readiness to impacts. This is, of course, a stylised representation. The overall size of the space economy grows in a given country as the "level of space activities" increases: a minimum of readiness factors are needed, such as budgets for R&D and human resources; this allows the intensity of a space programme to grow (more scientific missions, more patents, and/or more revenues generated by commercial space applications depending on the strategic objectives of the programme), thus leading to potentially more socio-economic impacts (*e.g.* productivity gains, regional economic growth).

The quality of available measures and comparable data for the space economy varies considerably throughout the input, output and impact stages. Some official statistical data are available for the readiness factors (*e.g.* space budgets, although not always readily comparable) and the intensity factors (*e.g.* number of space missions), but these need to be supplemented by private data sources (*e.g.* industry surveys) for revenues of the space sector. There are relatively less data on impacts, although the number and quality of datasets have improved since the early 2000s, as more countries study the impacts of their respective space sector on the wider economy.

Figure 1.1. **Development of the overall space economy**

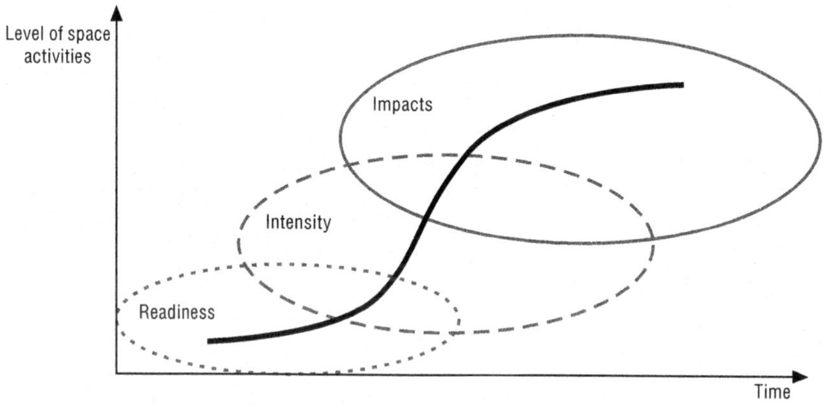

Source: Adapted from OECD (2011), *The Space Economy at a Glance 2011*, OECD Publishing, *http://dx.doi.org/10.1787/9789264111790-en*, p. 16.

In order to provide a better indication of the state of the space economy, more work on the concepts and definitions for the space sector and the wider space economy is needed. This calls for significant international co-operation, and the OECD Space Forum is working with the space community to provide a platform for such work.

References

OECD (2004), *Space 2030: The Future of Space Applications*, OECD Publishing, *http://dx.doi.org/10.1787/9789264020344-en*.

OECD (2005), *Space 2030: Tackling Society's Challenges*, OECD Publishing, *http://dx.doi.org/10.1787/9789264008342-en*.

OECD (2006), *Guide to Measuring the Information Society*, OECD Working Party on Indicators for the Information Society, Directorate for Science Technology and Industry, Committee for information, computer and communications policy, DSTI/IICP/IIS(2005)6/FINAL, Paris, 8 November.

OECD (2007), *The Space Economy at a Glance*, OECD Publishing, *http://dx.doi.org/10.1787/9789264040847-en*.

OECD (2008), *Space Technologies and Climate Change: Implications for Water Management, Marine Resources and Maritime Transport*, OECD Publishing, *http://dx.doi.org/10.1787/9789264054196-en*.

OECD (2011a), *OECD Guide to Measuring the Information Society 2011*, OECD Publishing, *http://dx.doi.org/10.1787/9789264113541-en*.

OECD (2011b), *The Space Economy at A Glance 2011*, OECD Publishing, *http://dx.doi.org/10.1787/9789264111790-en*.

PART I

Chapter 2

Definitions and Industrial Classifications

Chapter 2 provides answers to the following questions: What is the space economy? Where can one find data on space products and services in international and national statistical classification systems?

Definitions

An increasing number of countries are developing space systems and applications, but internationally agreed definitions for statistical terminology on space activities do not yet exist. This section takes stock of existing definitions for the space sector and the wider space economy.

Defining the space sector

There is not "one" space activity, but many space activities which extend into different fields of science and technology. The *Frascati Manual* provides a breakdown of existing science and technology fields, and space is present in several: astronomy (including astrophysics, space science); aerospace engineering; mechanical engineering; applied mechanics; thermodynamics; meteorology and atmospheric sciences, climatic research, to name just a few (see Annex C). In 2007, a revised version was adopted with the inclusion of many new fields (*e.g.* nanotechnology), with more breakdowns that take into account emerging and interdisciplinary fields, and for which internationally comparable data are sought (OECD, 2007b).

Technology-wise, the intrinsic overlaps between aerospace and core space technologies represent one of the first definitional challenges. The term "aerospace" describes "all the regions beyond the Earth's surface". One of the most complete definitions for the aerospace sector comes from Weiss and Amir (1999):

> The aerospace sector covers the "*assemblage of manufacturing that deal with vehicular flight within and beyond the Earth's atmosphere. The aerospace industry is engaged in the research, development, and manufacture of flight vehicles, including unpowered gliders and sailplanes, lighter-than-air craft, heavier-than-air craft (both fixed-wing and rotary wing), missiles, space launch vehicles, and spacecraft (manned and unmanned). Also included among its concerns are major flight-vehicle subsystems such as propulsion and avionics (aviation electronics) and key support systems necessary for the testing, operation, and maintenance of flight vehicles. In addition, the industry is engaged in the fabrication of non-aerospace products and systems that make use of aerospace technology.*

Based on the specificities of space activities, one generally accepted definition for the space sector is the following:

*The space sector includes all actors involved in the systematic application of engineering and scientific disciplines to the exploration and utilisation of outer space, an area which extends beyond the earth's atmosphere.**

This is a useful definition when trying to separate "aeronautics" and "space" activities. However, recent trends are showing the limits of the definition. The number of public and private actors involved in space activities worldwide has increased over the past decade and space applications have started permeating many different economic sectors. The space sector's definition, as mentioned above, has become too restrictive when trying to cover these new activities derived from space applications.

Defining the space economy

The space economy is much wider than the space sector, and can be defined using different angles. It can be defined by its products (*e.g.* satellites, launchers...), by its services (*e.g.* broadcasting, imagery/data delivery), by its programmatic objectives (*e.g.* military, robotic space exploration, human spaceflight, Earth observation, telecommunications...), by its actors/value chains (from R&D actors to users), and by its impacts (*e.g.* direct and indirect benefits...). One drawback is that narrow definitions might ignore important aspects, such as the R&D actors (laboratories and universities), the role of the military (as investor in R&D budgets and customer for space services), or ignore scientific and space exploration programmes altogether.

An example of a broad definition could be:

"The space economy covers the entire range of space activities and their spillovers, bringing knowledge and benefits to society at large."

NASA's Office of Strategic Communications also uses a relatively broad definition:

"The space economy: The full range of activities and the use of resources that create and provide value and benefits to human beings in the course of exploring, understanding and utilizing space." (NASA, 2007)

* Where does airspace end and where does space begin? This is not only a statistical issue as of mid-2011, there is no formally accepted legal delimitation of "outer space" internationally, although there is a growing corpus of norms and treaties dealing with space activities. As noted in OECD (2005), this may have implications for licensing regimes of new commercial launchers aiming to send payloads or paying passengers in orbit.

A narrower definition developed by the OECD Secretariat more targeted at value-chains is:

> *"The space economy includes: all public and private actors involved in developing and providing space-enabled products and services. It comprises a long value-added chain, starting with research and development actors and manufacturers of space hardware (e.g. launch vehicles, satellites, ground stations) and ending with the providers of space-enabled products (e.g. navigation equipment, satellite phones) and services (e.g. satellite-based meteorological services or direct-to-home video services) to final users."* (OECD, 2007c)

The OECD Space Forum participants established that the space economy should not be limited to just a few characteristics, because of the growing pervasiveness of space applications in many daily activities (meteorology, telecommunications...). Using lessons learned from other sectors (the information society notably), a broad definition of the space economy seemed appropriate, to encompass the different dimensions of programmes, services, actors. The following working definition is the starting point of the "*Handbook to Measuring the Space Economy*".

> *"The Space Economy is the full range of activities and the use of resources that create and provide value and benefits to human beings in the course of exploring, understanding, managing and utilising space. Hence, it includes all public and private actors involved in developing, providing and using space-related products and services, ranging from research and development, the manufacture and use of space infrastructure (ground stations, launch vehicles and satellites) to space-enabled applications (navigation equipment, satellite phones, meteorological services, etc.) and the scientific knowledge generated by such activities. It follows that the Space Economy goes well beyond the space sector itself, since it also comprises the increasingly pervasive and continually changing impacts (both quantitative and qualitative) of space-derived products, services and knowledge on economy and society."*

The space economy's value chain may vary, depending on the types of activities taking place in a given country. In general, the following components can be found:

- R&D Centres, laboratories, universities: whether they are public (*e.g.* technology centre of a space agency) or private establishments, they often play a key role in basic research and science, via contracts from government agencies.
- Manufacturers (satellites, launchers, ground segment): in addition to the large aerospace groups which tend to be active in the entire space manufacturing sector, smaller actors are active in specific manufacturing segments. An interesting trend since the early 2000s is the emergence of many small actors,

in parallel to the large groups (*e.g.* companies such as: Surrey Satellite Technology Ltd, OHB System AG).

- Operators including satellite signal providers (telecommunications, positioning), but also digital contents providers (*e.g.* satellite imagery). They increasingly tend also to be involved in the next segment of the value chain.
- Information services providers. They include not only information value-adders/integrators, but also actors in retail delivery. They work with ground equipment/devices developers.

Figure 2.1. **The space economy's simplified value chain**

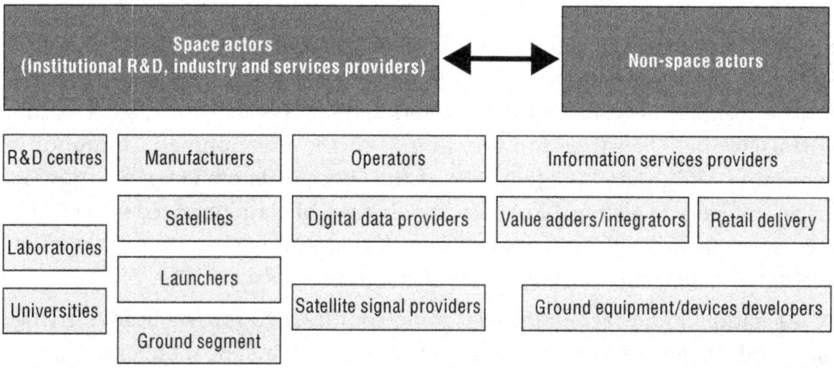

Source: Adapted from OECD (2011), *The Space Economy at a Glance 2011*, OECD Publishing, *http://dx.doi.org/10.1787/9789264111790-en*, p. 15.

The key actors in the space economy and different value chains will be discussed in more detail in Chapter 3.

Space in international classifications

There are a number of international and national classification systems in use. They structure industrial and economic activities in ways that facilitate comparison of national economic data on a year-by-year basis, or evaluate comparisons between countries. However, as this section will demonstrate, the diversity of space systems and applications explain the difficulty of pinpointing the space sector in existing industrial classifications.

Introducing industrial classifications

A classification is a "set of discrete, exhaustive and mutually exclusive observations, which can be assigned to one or more variables to be measured in the collation and/or presentation of data" (OECD, 2007a). The terms "classification" and "nomenclature" are often used interchangeably, despite the definition of a "nomenclature" being narrower than that of a "classification". Hierarchical classifications range from the broadest level (*e.g.* division) to the detailed level (*e.g.* class). Examples of classification include the United Nations International Standard Industrial Classification of All Economic Activities (ISIC, Revision 4), the statistical classification of economic activities in the European Community (NACE, Rev. 2), and the International Standard Classification of Occupations (ISCO-88).

Internationally, the current edition of ISIC (Rev. 4 released in 2008) includes most parts of the space sector under different aggregate categories. Even when just looking at high-technology categories, space products and services can be found in several sectors, mainly in aerospace, with some segments appearing in electronics and telecommunications and even armaments, since rockets are considered as weapons (*e.g.* missiles) in most countries (OECD, 2007c). There is no specific "space activity" classification in the ISIC, and disentangling the space sector from the larger aerospace and defence sectors remains a challenge in most countries. This is also true for other international classifications, such as the Central Product Classification (Version 2) or the Harmonized Commodity Description and Coding System (HS) of the World Customs Organization. A "space" category is also not found in the System of National Accounts (SNA). However, as we will see in the next sections, trade data are paradoxically often more detailed, in comparison to domestic industrial classifications.

At national and regional levels, some countries go further in identifying space products and services as economic activities, by adding more digits to the general international codes (*e.g.* France, United States). But this causes discrepancies when trying to compare the data internationally. This classification problem is not new; it occurs often with emerging economic sectors. Already in the late 1960s, at the beginning of the space age, the general "missiles and spacecraft" statistical category was identified as causing methodological difficulties in the United States when trying to assess aerospace prices over time because of the heterogeneity of the products covered in the single category (Campbell, 1970).

The International Standard Industrial Classification (ISIC)

ISIC consists of a coherent and consistent classification structure of economic activities based on a set of internationally agreed concepts, definitions, principles and classification rules. These economic activities are subdivided in a hierarchical, four-level structure of mutually exclusive categories. The current edition of ISIC (Rev. 4) includes most parts of the space sector under different aggregate categories. Indeed, there is no specific "space activity" classification in the ISIC, and disentangling the space sector from the larger aerospace sector remains a challenge in most countries. Despite differences in activities (manufacturing an aircraft vs. manufacturing a space launcher or a satellite), it remains arduous to disentangle industrial activities which are often conducted by the same industrial groups.

Box 2.1. **A closer look at ISIC Class 3030: Manufacture of air and spacecraft and related machinery**

Section: C – Manufacturing

Division: 30 – Manufacture of other transport equipment

Group: 303 – Manufacture of air and spacecraft and related machinery

Class: 3030 – Manufacture of air and spacecraft and related machinery

This class includes:

- Manufacture of airplanes for the transport of goods or passengers, for use by the defence forces, for sport or other purposes.
- Manufacture of helicopters.
- Manufacture of gliders, hang-gliders.
- Manufacture of dirigibles and hot air balloons.
- Manufacture of parts and accessories of the aircraft of this class:
  - major assemblies such as fuselages, wings, doors, control surfaces, landing gear, fuel tanks, nacelles, etc.
  - airscrews, helicopter rotors and propelled rotor blades;
  - motors and engines of a kind typically found on aircraft;
  - parts of turbojets and turboprops for aircraft.
- Manufacture of ground flying trainers.
- Manufacture of spacecraft and launch vehicles, satellites, planetary probes, orbital stations, shuttles.
- Manufacture of intercontinental ballistic missiles (ICBM).

This class also includes:

- overhaul and conversion of aircraft or aircraft engines;
- manufacture of aircraft seats.

This class excludes:

- manufacture of telecommunication equipment for satellites (class 2630);
- manufacture of aircraft instrumentation and aeronautical instruments (class 2651);
- manufacture of air navigation systems (class 2651);
- manufacture of lighting equipment for aircraft (class 2740);
- manufacture of ignition parts and other electrical parts for internal combustion engines (class 2790);
- manufacture of pistons, piston rings and carburetors (class 2811);
- manufacture of aircraft launching gear, aircraft carrier catapults and related equipment (class 2829).

Source: Adapted from United Nations (2010), *International Standard Industrial Classification (ISIC) Rev. 4*, United Nations, New York, *http://unstats.un.org/unsd/cr/registry/isic-4.asp, Accessed on 4 January.*

A major cause of inconsistency among economic statistics is that surveys and statistics for different industries or activities are designed independently of each other (United Nations Statistical Commission, 2007). This is also the case for the space sector. Although current industrial classifications have limitations, several industry surveys are conducted annually in Europe, North America and Asia using very different definitions. These surveys provide useful data on the industry, as they fill gaps in official statistics, but international comparability between surveys can be limited, as discussed in the table below. Examples of surveys are provided in national sections.

Table 2.1. **Main advantages and inconveniences of using industrial classifications *vs.* specialised industry surveys**

	PROS	CONS
Industrial classification approach	Ability to compare different territories, years, industries, etc. Methods documented, reliability of data.	Disaggregation is limited by the existing industrial codes. Dissemination of data is submitted to confidentiality (if just a few companies appear). The sectors are harder to define and might be underestimated/overestimated by the exclusion/inclusion of enterprises belonging to other industries. The time adjustments to changes in the economy for emerging new industries are very long compared to the approach based on industry surveys.
Targeted industry surveys	Allows the inclusion of different businesses, even if a priori they belong to another industry. Faster collection and availability of data. Circumvents some problems related to confidentiality.	Comparability difficult (territories, years, industries). Total number of companies underestimated/ overestimated (not exhaustive). For the production of statistics, the survey response rate may be low, as companies are not obliged to respond. The data may be unreliable given the different methods of collection.

Source: Adapted from Institut de la Statistique du Québec (2009), *Profil statistique de l'industrie aérospatiale*, Gouvernement du Québec, Quebec, October.

The Central Product Classification and the Harmonized System

In parallel to ISIC industrial classifications, a number of dedicated classifications exist to track international trade data. They are the Central Product Classification (CPC, Version 2) and the Harmonized Commodity Description and Coding System (HS).

The CPC constitutes a comprehensive classification of all goods and services, describing the output of each economic activity by product. The HS is an international nomenclature set up by the World Customs Organization for the classification of products to facilitate customs purposes, with some 5 300 product descriptions. Both systems include a number of space products and services, but usually at an aggregated level (see Table). However, based on these industry trade classifications, countries tend to create very detailed subcategories for their different products at the national level. As an example, the United States' International Trade Administration provides more detailed

Table 2.2. **Selected space activities in international classifications**

ACTIVITY	CPC Ver. 2[1]	ISIC 4	SITC Rev. 4	HS 2007
Manufacturing and launch services	49630 Launch vehicles for satellites	3030	792.5	8802.60
	65320 Space transport services, freight (*i.e.* Launching of satellites into space)	5120	792.5	–
	64250 Space transport services of passengers	5110	792.5	–
	67640 Supporting services for space transport	5223	792.5	–
	88824 Air and spacecraft manufacturing services	3030	792.5	–
Insurance	71332 Marine, aviation, and other transport insurance services (Includes "satellite launching insurance policies, underwriting of")	6512	–	–
Earth observation and navigation	83430 Weather forecasting and meteorological services (more than satellite data activities)	7490	–	–
	83421 Surface surveying (includes surveying by satellite)	7110	–	–
	84190 Other telecommunications services (includes Satellite tracking services)	6110	–	–
Telecommunications	48220 Radar apparatus, radio navigational aid apparatus and radio remote control apparatus (includes "satellite linked auto security device used to send signals via satellite to a specific vehicle to carry out electromechanical commands on that vehicle based on an encoded signal)	2651	764.83	8526
	49630 Satellites, telecommunications	3030	792.5	8802.60
	54614 Residential antenna installation services (includes Installation of satellite dishes)	4321	–	–
	84131 Mobile telecommunications services – access and use (includes satellite telephone services)	6120	–	–
	84150 Data transmission services (includes satellite space segment, occasional use feeds, broadcast applications, VSAT satellite service, occasional use, broadcast or two-way applications)	6110	–	
	84634 Home programme distribution services, pay per view (includes pay-per-view television program, by satellite (*i.e.* Video-on-demand, by satellite)	6010 6020	–	–
	91134 Public administrative services related to transport and communications (includes administrative services related to satellite communications)	8413	–	–
	Subclass: 47223 – Other telephone sets and apparatus for transmission or reception of voice, images or other data, including apparatus for communication in a wired or wireless network (such as a local or wide area network) (includes: Field telephones (military))	2610 2630	764.11	8517.18 8517.61 8517.62 8517.69

1. The classifications codes usually all include more than just the space products and services indicated.

Source: Adapted from United Nations (2010), International Standard Industrial Classification (ISIC) Rev. 4, United Nations, New York, *http://unstats.un.org/unsd/cr/registry/isic-4.asp*, Accessed on 4 January.

categories for exports and imports of aerospace vehicles and equipment (*e.g.* Communications satellites category), compared to the Census Bureau's data on the production of the domestic industry (see Section 2.3 on the United States).

The HS and CPC classifications are also particularly useful tools for countries which regulate the trade of strategic commodities for national security purposes and international security arrangements. Whenever countries set up specific "Munitions List" and "Dual-use Goods List", as in the case of the United States, France or Canada, the use of common nomenclatures

Box 2.2. **Space technologies and the Missile Technology Control Regime**

The Missile Technology Control Regime (MTCR) is an informal political understanding among states seeking to limit the proliferation of missiles and missile technology, which can be used for the delivery of all types of weapons of mass destruction (WMD). The regime was formed in 1987 by the G7 industrialised countries (Canada, France, Germany, Italy, Japan, the United Kingdom, and the United States). There are currently 34 member countries (Partners) of the MTCR.*

The Regime places particular focus on rockets and unmanned aerial vehicles:

- Category I items include complete rocket and unmanned aerial vehicle systems (including ballistic missiles, space launch vehicles, sounding rockets, cruise missiles, target drones, and reconnaissance drones), capable of delivering a payload of at least 500 kg to a range of at least 300 km, their major complete subsystems (such as rocket stages, engines, guidance sets, and re-entry vehicles), and related software and technology, as well as specially designed production facilities for these items. Pursuant to the MTCR Guidelines, exports of Category I items are subject to an unconditional strong presumption of denial regardless of the purpose of the export and are licensed for export only on rare occasions. Additionally, exports of production facilities for Category I items are absolutely prohibited.
- Category II items include other less-sensitive and dual-use missile related components, as well as other complete missile systems capable of a range of at least 300 km, regardless of payload. Their export is subject to licensing requirements taking into consideration the non-proliferation factors specified in the MTCR Guidelines. Exports judged by the exporting country to be intended for use in WMD delivery are to be subjected to a strong presumption of denial.

* Argentina (1993); Australia (1990); Austria (1991); Belgium (1990); Brazil (1995); Bulgaria (2004); Canada (1987); Czech Republic (1998); Denmark (1990); Finland (1991); France (1987); Germany (1987); Greece 1992); Hungary (1993); Iceland (1993); Ireland (1992); Italy (1987); Japan (1987); Luxemburg (1990); Netherlands (1990); New Zealand (1991); Norway (1990); Poland (1998); Portugal (1992); Republic of Korea (2001); Russian Federation (1995); South Africa (1995); Spain (1990); Sweden (1991); Switzerland (1992); Turkey (1997); Ukraine (1998); United Kingdom (1987); United States of America (1987). The date in brackets represents the initial year of membership.

Source: Adapted from: The Missile Technology Control Regime (MTCR) MTCR *website*, Washington, DC. Available: *www.mtcr.info/english/FAQ-E.html* [*Accessed January*].

contributes to control international transfers of sensitive technologies. Space technologies, being dual by nature, are often included in these restrictive trade regimes (see Box 2.2). This particular framework explains why commercial space products are sometimes misrepresented in official trade statistics (*e.g.* components of satellites, entire systems not visible statistically). But in some cases, the exported space products can easily be found in arms trade statistics (see Chapter 6 for more on trade).

Review of selected national/regional classifications

The following sections review the national classifications of a number of countries/regions. They include actors with major space programmes: the United States and Canada, Europe and France.

North-America

The North American Industry Classification System (NAICS) provides a consistent system for economic analysis across the three North American Free Trade Agreement partners – Canada, Mexico and the United States. The North American Product Classification System (NAPCS) will complement this system in time. Both the United States and Canada have had established space industries for decades.

Space activities can be found in two main family codes: "Manufacturing" and "Information", but as in other national classifications, the level of aggregation is problematic. Already in the late 1960s, the first reports and recommendations concerning economic statistics on the aerospace sector were published in the United States. A call for more detailed statistics was spurred by the need to better estimate the aerospace purchases made by the US Air Force over time (Campbell, 1970). The "missiles and spacecraft" statistical category was identified as causing methodological difficulties when trying to assess aerospace prices overtime, because of the heterogeneity of the products covered in the single category. As shown in the next table, there are many NAICS codes which include space activities. Some codes go so far as to aggregate even further some ISIC categories to facilitate the inclusion of all actors involved in the activity (see for example the NAICS, Code 334220, for satellite telecommunications manufacturing). Looking at the broader space activities, however it remains difficult to isolate satellites from the different Guided Missile and Space Vehicle categories.

The US Census Bureau publishes an Annual Survey of Manufactures (ASM) which features aerospace companies, and measures industry outputs, inputs, and operating status. The survey also includes statistics on employment, hours worked, selected operating expenses, value added by manufacturing, capital expenditures, and energy consumption, to name but a

Table 2.3. **List of NAICS Codes and ISIC 4 equivalence for space activities**

NAICS Codes	Description	ISIC
Government		
927110 Space Research and Technology	Government establishments primarily[3] engaged in the administration and operations of space flights, space research, and space exploration. Included in this industry are government establishments operating space flight centres.	5120 and 8413
Manufacturing		
336414 Guided Missile and Space Vehicle Manufacturing	Establishments primarily engaged in 1) manufacturing complete guided missiles and space vehicles and/or 2) developing and making prototypes of guided missiles or space vehicles.	3030
336415 Guided Missile and Space Vehicle Propulsion Unit and Propulsion Unit Parts Manufacturing	Establishments primarily engaged in 1) manufacturing guided missile and/or space vehicle propulsion units and propulsion unit parts and/or 2) developing and making prototypes of guided missile and space vehicle propulsion units and propulsion unit parts.	3030
336419 Other Guided Missile and Space Vehicle Parts and Auxiliary Equipment Manufacturing	Establishments primarily engaged in1) manufacturing guided missile and space vehicle parts and auxiliary equipment (except guided missile and space vehicle propulsion units and propulsion unit parts) and/or 2) developing and making prototypes of guided missile and space vehicle parts and auxiliary equipment. Selected corresponding Index Entries: • Guided missile and space vehicle parts (except engines) manufacturing. • Airframe assemblies for guided missiles manufacturing. • Space capsules manufacturing.	3030
334220 Radio and Television Broadcasting and Wireless Communications Equipment Manufacturing	Establishments primarily engaged in manufacturing radio and television broadcast and wireless communications equipment. Examples of products made by these establishments are: transmitting and receiving antennas, cable television equipment, GPS equipment, pagers, cellular phones, mobile communications equipment, and radio and television studio and broadcasting equipment. Selected corresponding Index Entries: • Global positioning system (GPS) equipment manufacturing. • Earth station communications equipment manufacturing. • Satellite communications equipment manufacturing. • Satellite antennas manufacturing. • Telephones, cellular, manufacturing.	2630 and 2651[1]
334511 Search, Detection, Navigation, Guidance, Aeronautical, and Nautical System and Instrument Manufacturing	Establishments primarily engaged in manufacturing search, detection, navigation, guidance, aeronautical, and nautical systems and instruments. Examples of products made by these establishments are aircraft instruments (except engine), flight recorders, navigational instruments and systems, radar systems and equipment, and sonar systems and equipment. Selected corresponding Index Entries: • Gyroscopes manufacturing. • Radio magnetic instrumentation (RMI) manufacturing. • Space vehicle guidance systems and equipment manufacturing.	2651
334519 Other Measuring and Controlling Device Manufacturing	Manufacturing of aircraft engine instruments, meteorological systems and equipment.	2651
Services		
481212 Nonscheduled chartered freight air transportation	Establishments primarily engaged in providing air transportation of cargo without transporting passengers with no regular routes and regular schedules. This includes space transportation, freight, nonscheduled.	5120
238290 Other Building Equipment Contractors	Establishments engaged in the installation of residential satellite dishes.	4321

Table 2.3. **List of NAICS Codes and ISIC 4 equivalence for space activities** *(cont.)*

NAICS Codes	Description	ISIC
517410 Satellite Telecommunications	Establishments primarily engaged in providing telecommunications services to other establishments in the telecommunications and broadcasting industries by forwarding and receiving communications signals via a system of satellites or reselling satellite telecommunications. Selected corresponding Index Entries: • Earth stations for satellite communication carriers. • Long-distance telephone satellite communication carriers. • Resellers, satellite telecommunication. • Satellite telecommunication carriers. • Satellite telecommunication resellers. • Telephone communications carriers, satellite.	6130 and 6190[2]
517110 Wired Telecommunications Carriers	Establishments primarily engaged in providing direct-to-home satellite television services to individual households or consumers.	6130
515111 Radio Networks:	Establishments primarily engaged in assembling and transmitting aural programming to their affiliates or subscribers via over-the-air broadcasts, cable, or satellite. The programming covers a wide variety of material, such as news services, religious programming, weather, sports, or music.	6130
R&D establishments		
541712 Research and Development in the Physical, Engineering, and Life Sciences	Establishments conducting research and experimental development, including R&D establishments engaged in guided missile and space vehicle R&D (except prototype production).	7210

1. The NAICS Code 334220 aggregates ISIC Class 2651 (which includes GPS equipment and satellite manufacturing) and ISIC 2651.
2. The NAICS Code 517410 aggregates ISIC Class 6130 and 6190 (which includes satellite telecommunications resellers)
3. An establishments primarily engaged on an activity is one whose principal activity is in one of the designated ISIC groups. Such an establishment may also have a secondary activity in a different ISIC group.

Source: Adapted from US Census Bureau (2011), North American Industry Classification System (NAICS), website, Washington, DC. Available: www.census.gov/eos/www/naics/ [Accessed January].

few. It also provides estimates of value of shipments for over 1 400 classes of manufactured products (US Census Bureau, 2008a). The information is updated from two sources: the Internal Revenue Service administrative records and the Company Organization Survey.

In terms of trade statistics, about 500 of the 22 000 commodity classification codes used in reporting US merchandise trade are identified as "advanced technology" codes (US Census Bureau, 2008b). These codes are used for advanced technology products that meet several criteria, such as belonging to a recognized high technology field (*e.g.* aerospace), representing leading edge technology in that field (see Box 2.3). This product and commodity-based measure of advanced technology differs from broader NAICS industry-based measures which include all goods produced by a particular industry group, regardless of the level of technology embodied in the goods.

As mentioned previously on industry trade classifications, countries tend to create detailed subcategories for their different products at the national level to facilitate tracking of their exports and imports. This is the case of US

Box 2.3. **General advanced technology products in US trade statistics**

About 500 commodity classification codes used in reporting US merchandise trade are identified as "advanced technology" codes. Below are three categories which include space-related commodities:

Code 04: "Information & Communications"

This category focuses on products that are able to process increased volumes of information in shorter periods of time. Includes central processing units, all computers and some peripheral units such as disk drive units and control units, along with modems, facsimile machines and telephonic switching apparatus. Examples of other products included are radar apparatus and communication satellites. The codes pertinent for space include:

- 04 8529904740 Radio Navigational Aid Apparatus Parts
- 04 8802603000 Communications Satellites
- 04 8803903000 Parts of Communications Satellites

Code 08: "Aerospace"

This category encompasses most new military and civil helicopters, airplanes and spacecraft (with the exception of communications satellites that are included under Information & Communications Technology). Other products included are turbojet aircraft engines, flight simulators and automatic pilots. The codes pertinent for space include:

- 08 880260 Spacecraft (including satellites) and suborbital and space-craft launch vehicles
- 08 8802603000 Communications satellites
- 08 8803903000 Parts of communications satellites
- 08 8802609020 Military Spacecraft & Launch Vehicle (Excluding Communications Satellite)
- 08 8802609040 Non-Military Spacecraft & Launch Vehicle (Excluding Communications Satellite)

Code 09: "Weapons"

This category primarily encompasses products with military application, and includes such products as guided missiles and parts, bombs, torpedoes, mines, missiles, rocket launchers and some firearms. The codes pertinent for space include:

- 9014204000 Automatic Pilots for Aeronautical/Space Navigation
- 9014206000 Electrical Instrument, Aeronautical or Space Navigation
- 9014208080 Instrument & appliances, Aeronautical/Space Navigation, NESOI (Not Elsewhere Specified or Included in trade exports, customs)
- 9027504050 Photometers

Source: US Census Bureau (2008b) *Foreign Trade Statistics – Advanced Technology Product Definitions*, Washington, DC Available: *www.census.gov/* [*Accessed June*].

statistics. The International Trade Administration provides more detailed categories for exports and imports of aerospace vehicles and equipment (*e.g.* communications satellites category), compared to the Census Bureau's data on the domestic industry (US International Trade Administration, 2011).

American trade statistics are initially collected and compiled in terms of approximately 8 000 commodity classifications in the "Statistical Classification of Domestic and Foreign Commodities Exported from the United States" (dubbed "Schedule B" by the Trade Administration). For space products and services, these commodity classifications are quasi-similar to the ones found in the General Advanced Technology Products, described above. In practice, official data for the domestic space industry (based on ISIC/NAICS classifications) are less detailed, and may not exactly correspond to the trade statistics because of slightly broader coverage.

In that context, industry associations (US Aerospace Industry Association, Satellite Industry Association) and their contractors tend to use some definitions and data from the US Department of Commerce, but in priority use their own estimates, when presenting the state of the US space sector (AIA, 2011).

Europe

The NACE system ("Nomenclature statistique des activités économiques dans la Communauté européenne") is the statistical classification of economic activities in the European Community. In the European Union, NACE is used uniformly within all the member states, which may use their own national classification to derive subclasses. As in the case of the North American NAICS, space is closely intertwined with the aeronautic sector, as shown in Table 2.4.

With respect to trade, European countries use the European Combined Nomenclature (CN), which includes the international Harmonized System (HS) classifications with further Community subdivisions. A number of categories are directly applicable to a number of space products and services, as shown in Box 2.4.

Using the different classifications, Eurostat publishes data on the European aerospace sector (Eurostat, 2006). Most statistics remain highly aggregated, with the space industry being included in the larger aerospace categories. In parallel to Eurostat's official statistics, the space industry association Eurospace publishes an annual report (Eurospace, 2010). One major advantage of the Eurospace surveys is the transparent methodological process used to collect and report industry data.

Table 2.4. **List of NACE Codes and ISIC 4 equivalence for space activities**

NACE 2 Codes	Description	ISIC
Manufacturing		
3030 Manufacture of air and spacecraft and related machinery	This class includes (among others) the manufacture of spacecraft and launch vehicles, satellites, planetary probes, orbital stations, shuttles.	3030
3316 Repair and maintenance of aircraft and spacecraft	This class includes the repair and maintenance of aircraft and spacecraft.	3315
2630 Manufacture of communications equipment	This class includes the manufacture of telephone and data communications equipment used to move signals electronically (*e.g.* ground equipment for satellites communications).	2630
2651 Manufacture of instruments and appliances for measuring, testing and navigation	This class includes (among others): • manufacture of search, detection, navigation, aeronautical, and nautical equipment, including sonobuoys; • manufacture of radar equipment; • manufacture of GPS devices.	2651
Services		
4321 Specialised construction activities	This class includes different types of electrical installation, including satellite dishes.	4321
5122 Space transport	This class includes: • launching of satellites and space vehicles; • space transport of freight and passengers.	5122
6010 and 6020 Radio and TV broadcasting	Both classes include the operations and maintenance of switching and transmission facilities to provide point to point communications via landlines, microwave or a combination of landlines and satellite linkups.	6010 6020
6130 Satellite telecommunications activities	This class includes: • operating, maintaining or providing access to facilities for the transmission of voice, data, text, sound and video using a satellite telecommunications infrastructure; • delivery of visual, aural or textual programming received from cable networks, local television stations or radio networks to consumers via direct-to-home satellite systems (The units classified here do not generally originate programming material). This class also includes: • provision of Internet access by the operator of the satellite infrastructure. This class excludes: • telecommunications resellers (Class 61.90).	6130
6190 Other telecommunications activities	This class includes (among others): • provision of specialised telecommunications applications, such as satellite tracking, communications telemetry, and radar station operations; • operation of satellite terminal stations and associated facilities operationally connected with one or more terrestrial communications systems and capable of transmitting telecommunications to or receiving telecommunications from satellite systems; • provision of Internet access over networks between the client and the ISP not owned or controlled by the ISP, such as dial-up Internet access? etc.	6190
8422 Defence activities	This class includes (among others): • administration, supervision and operation of military defence affairs and land, sea, air and *space defence forces* (including research and development policies and related funds).	8422

Source: Adapted from Eurostat (2011), *Eurostat's Combined Nomenclature*, RAMON Eurostat's Metadata Server, Brussels. Available: *http://ec.europa.eu/eurostat/ramon* [*Accessed February*].

Box 2.4. **Selected categories in Eurostat's Combined Nomenclature (CN)**

SECTION XVII – Vehicles, Aircraft, Vessels And Associated Transport Equipment

Chapter 88 – Aircraft, Spacecraft, And Parts Thereof

8801 Balloons and dirigibles; gliders, hang gliders and other non-powered aircraft

8802 Other aircraft (for example, helicopters, aeroplanes); spacecraft (including satellites) and suborbital and spacecraft launch vehicles

88026010 Spacecraft, including satellites

88026090 Suborbital and spacecraft launch vehicles

8803 Parts of goods of heading 8801 or 8802

88039020 Parts of spacecraft, including Satellites, n.e.s.

88039030 Parts of suborbital and spacecraft launch vehicles, n.e.s.

SECTION XIX – Arms And Ammunition; Parts And Accessories Thereof

93 Chapter 93 – Arms And Ammunition; Parts And Accessories Thereof

9301 Military weapons, other than revolvers, pistols (and the arms of heading 9307)

9306 Bombs, grenades, torpedoes, mines, missiles and similar munitions of war and parts thereof

Source: Adapted from Eurostat (2011), *Eurostat's Combined Nomenclature*, RAMON Eurostat's Metadata Server, Brussels. Available: *http://ec.europa.eu/eurostat/ramon* [*Accessed February*].

France

France bases its statistical classifications on the General Industrial Classification of Economic Activities within the European Communities (NACE). The main NACE categories are then broken down further in the French national statistical system NAF (*Nomenclature d'Activités Française*) (Madinier, 2009). As in other countries, statistics on the space sector are often "lost" in aggregated aerospace figures. However, the French statistical classification system provides a notable level of detail for space activities.

Official French statistics tend to focus on manufacturing more than services. The national statistical office INSEE (Institut national de la statistique et des études économiques) conducts regional surveys in the Midi-Pyrenees region (annually since 1982), Aquitaine (annually since 2000), and French Guiana (regularly, but not annually), specifically covering manufacturers, subcontractors and service providers in the aeronautical and space sectors. The surveys provide snapshots of the French aerospace

Table 2.5. **Statistical classification equivalences for selected space activities: International, North-American and European classifications**

Space aActivity	International (ISIC Rev. 4)	North America (NAICS 2007)	Europe (NACE Version 2)
Manufacturing of space products	Class 3030: Manufacture of air and spacecraft and related machinery Class: 3315 – Repair of transport equipment, except motor vehicles	336414 Guided Missile and Space Vehicle Manufacturing 334511 Space vehicle guidance systems and equipment manufacturing 336415 Guided Missile and Space Vehicle Propulsion Unit and Propulsion Unit Parts Manufacturing 336419 Other Guided Missile and Space Vehicle Parts and Auxiliary Equipment Manufacturing	303 – Manufacture of air and spacecraft and related machinery 3316 – Repair and maintenance of aircraft and spacecraft
Space transport	Class: 5120 – Freight air transport (includes – launching of satellites and space vehicles; space transport)	336414 Guided Missile and Space Vehicle Manufacturing	512 – Freight air transport and space transport 5122 – Space transport
Telecommunications	Class 6120: Wireless telecommunications activities Class 6130: Satellite telecommunications activities Class: 4321 – Electrical installation (includes satellite dishes)	517410 Satellite Telecommunications 515111 Satellite radio networks	612 Wireless telecommunications activities 6130 Satellite telecommunications activities
Remote sensing and navigation	Class 2670: Manufacture of optical instruments and photographic equipment Class 2680: Manufacture of magnetic and optical media Class 2651: Manufacture of measuring, testing, navigating and control equipment 2652 – Manufacture of watches and clocks Class: 7110 – Architectural and engineering activities and related technical consultancy (collection of data by satellite)	334220 Global positioning system (GPS) equipment manufacturing	267 – Manufacture of optical instruments and photographic equipment 268 – Manufacture of magnetic and optical media 265 – Manufacture of instruments and appliances for measuring, testing and navigation; watches and clocks 2651 – Manufacture of instruments and appliances for measuring, testing and navigation 2652 – Manufacture of watches and clocks
Weapons (*e.g.* rocket launchers)	Class 2520: Manufacture of weapons and ammunition Class 3040: Manufacture of military fighting vehicles	336414 Guided Missile and Space Vehicle Manufacturing	C25.4 – Manufacture of weapons and ammunition C30.4 – Manufacture of military fighting vehicles

industry, an important sector for the economies of the three regions in terms of revenues and employment. The surveys are limited to current industry classifications and exclude other actors involved in services. For space activities, Category "3030" in the NACE system (Revision 2) covers "Manufacture of air and spacecraft and related machinery" (Construction aéronautique et spatiale). The French NAF provides a more detailed category with the 35.3C code: Manufacturing of launchers and space vehicles (*Construction de lanceurs et engins spatiaux*).

One useful advance for French industry surveys would be to use the detailed subcategories that already exist at the NAF level. They are for example:

- Product 00020: Manufacturing of Ariane 5 launchers (*Construction de lanceurs Ariane* 5).
- Product 00021: Parts of launchers, including boosters (*Parties de Lanceurs, y compris booster*).
- Product 00022: Other launchers aside from Ariane 5, *e.g.* M51, M52, etc. (*Autres lanceurs qu'Ariane* 5 *M51, M52, etc.*).
- Product 00030: Manufacturing of space vehicles (*Construction d'engins spatiaux*).
- Product 000301: Space vehicles and satellites (*Engins spatiaux et satellites*).
- Product 000302: Parts of space vehicles and satellites (*Parties d'engins spatiaux et satellites*).

Envisaging ISIC reclassification and alternative measures

The disentangling or disaggregating of the space data within the ISIC Rev. 4 classification system is one of the major challenges for users seeking official statistics on the space sector. There are three possible avenues to overcome the current limitations of current industrial classifications. The first one would be to maintain the status-quo and rely on best efforts of data providers; the second, more radical, would be to modify the current industrial classifications; and the final option would be to start a statistical rapprochement with a number of selected countries via industry mapping.

Option 1: Maintain status quo: The first option would be to leave the situation as it is, not resolving the outstanding issues that have been identified throughout the previous sections.

As the space industry continues to grow with technological advances and propagation of products and services (*e.g.* navigation aids), it might be worthwhile to pause and examine how the industry might develop further in the future before putting considerable effort towards classifying it.

However, obtaining data on manufacturing and services derived from the space industry may become indispensable. The option of not taking action in trying to resolve issues related to the reclassification of manufacturing in aerospace would prolong the eventual need to do so later, when even more actors will be using their own classifications and this would make the harmonisation process more difficult.

Option 2: Changing the current industrial classifications: As seen previously, space products and services are usually included in wider ISIC categories, where space products tend to account for a small proportion of the total. The possibility to create specific categories for space-products and services could be a possible solution (*e.g.* creating new ISIC subcategories dubbed "launchers manufacturing" and "satellite manufacturing").

During the last major ISIC 4 revision, the Class 6410 (*Satellite Telecommunications and Navigation Services*) in ISIC Rev. 3.1 was changed, and a separate ISIC Class was created for satellite telecommunications (*Class 6130: Satellite telecommunications activities*). This class now includes activities of "operating, maintaining or providing access to facilities for the transmission of voice, data, text, sound, and video using a satellite telecommunications infrastructure".

Separating other specific space activities from the larger aerospace categories could be possible by analysing the many detailed subcategories that have been created so far in national classifications. This process would require a careful examination of the space and aeronautics industry to see which items should be classified where. It might be however a time-consuming process that may require some compromises, as shown in the next table.

Table 2.6. **Modifying future ISIC classifications: Pros and Cons**

PROS	CONS
Comparability: Data would be comparable among all countries that are able to provide statistics. **Definitions:** Concepts, definitions would be agreed on by public authorities, thus contributing to better international comparisons (industry/private data sources, would also benefit from the process). **Learning Process:** Even if the process is lengthy, it would allow participants to have a better understanding of the economic dimensions of the space sector and its many derived activities (*e.g.* navigation).	**Political:** Needs clear political support, as this is an undertaking involving many actors (statistical offices, governmental agencies, space community). **Time Consuming:** ISIC revisions take time (reclassifications occur every several years), with compromises to come to an agreement on concepts and detailed classifications. **No Data:** Some countries may not want to have discussions about classifications, as not all countries have space programmes and if they do, they may have confidentiality issues.

Option 3: Start a statistical rapprochement with a number of selected countries via industry mapping: A third interim solution would be to build on existing codes to advance international comparability. This could be done by encouraging statistical rapprochement between selected countries, using the same lower digit codes and definitions, and gathering data through common industry surveys using the same key questions. Such efforts could also be encouraged by the private sector, particularly through aerospace industry associations agreeing on a number of key definitions.

Co-operation is already taking place via the OECD Space Forum activities and the regular meetings of the International Astronautical Federation's Space Economy Technical Committee. This committee was created in 2008 within the International Astronautical Federation to tackle the issue of comparability of economic data on the space sector. Ultimately, a move to change international classifications for an increasing number of space activities could contribute to increased clarity. As seen before, this already occurred during the ISIC Revision 4, which created a new and separate ISIC Class specifically for satellite telecommunications activities.

Already a number of countries provide lower digit categories in their own classifications. The objective would be to ensure rapprochement of definitions between data suppliers, including government departments (*e.g.* national statistical offices, national space agencies) or private players, such as industry associations. A particular advantage of this method is that many countries already have official estimates relating to outputs of the space sector. For example, the United Kingdom, France, Canada, Norway and to some degree Italy already provide official estimates concerning their space sector and its output of goods and services. However, this alternative requires consultation of various possible providers/collectors of data. Table 2.7 summarises the pros and cons of this approach.

Table 2.7. **Pros and Cons of starting a statistical rapprochement with a number of selected countries**

PROS	CONS
Comprehensive approach: Agreement on definitions of a wide variety of goods and services. **Available:** Many organisations already collect space industry data annually including goods & services. **Consistency:** Can work with data providers to ensure quality data through the use of best practices or some commonalities in terms of concepts, definitions, classifications and methodologies. **Important learning tool:** Even if the discussions fail to produce a sound result, they could lead to more awareness of the space industry and its issues. **Expansion:** The process can be extended to many OECD and non-OECD countries (*e.g.* India, China).	**Agreement Required:** Would require agreement on concepts, definitions, classifications and methodologies. While this may seem simple, the process may become quite complicated with each member going back to their national space players (government and industry) and determining what they can provide. **Data Disparity:** May cause discrepancy between the countries which started the rapprochement and the ones which didn't. **Confidentiality:** How to handle data confidentiality issues: *i.e.* what if there are only a few companies in some countries?

References

AIA (Aerospace Industry Association) (2011), *US Aerospace Statistics, website*, Washington, DC. Available: *www.aia-aerospace.org/economics/aerospace_statistics/* [*Accessed 10 March*].

Campbell, H.G. (1970), *Aerospace Price Indexes*, RAND Corporation, Report Prepared for the US Air Force, Washington, DC, December.

Eurospace (2010), *The European Space Industry in 2009, Facts & Figures*, 14th edition, Paris, August.

Eurostat (2006), *Manufacture of aerospace equipment in the European Union*, Issue No. 7/2006, Brussels, February.

Eurostat (2011), *Eurostat's Combined Nomenclature*, RAMON Eurostat's Metadata Server, Brussels. Available: *http://ec.europa.eu/eurostat/ramon* [*Accessed February*].

Institut de la Statistique du Québec (2009), *Profil statistique de l'industrie aérospatiale*, Gouvernement du Québec, Quebec, October.

Madinier, C. (2009), "The aggregated classifications of NAF Rev. 21", *Courrier des statistiques*, English series, No. 15.

OECD (2007a), *OECD Glossary of Statistical Terms, webpage*, Paris, France. Available: *http://stats.oecd.org/glossary* [*Accessed 6 June 2007*].

OECD (2007b), *Revised Field of Science and Technology (FOS) Classification in the Frascati Manual*, Directorate for Science, Technology and Industry, Committee for Scientific and Technological Policy, Working Party of National Experts on Science and Technology Indicators, OECD, DSTI/EAS/STP/NESTI(2006)19/FINAL, Paris.

OECD (2007c), *The Space Economy at a Glance*, OECD Publishing.

The Missile Technology Control Regime (MTCR) (2011), *MTCR website*, Washington, DC. Available: *www.mtcr.info/english/FAQ-E.html* [*Accessed January*].

United Nations (2010), *International Standard Industrial Classification (ISIC) Rev. 4*, United Nations, New York, website: *http://unstats.un.org/unsd/cr/registry/isic-4.asp, Accessed on 4 January*.

United Nations Statistical Commission (2007), *Friends of the Chair on integrated economic statistics, Items for discussion and decision: integrated economic statistics*, United Nations Economic and Social Council, Statistical Commission, Thirty-ninth session, Item 3 (e) of the provisional agenda, 26-29 February 2008, E/CN.3/2008/6, New York, 12 December.

US Census Bureau (2008a), *Economic Programs Overview: Annual Survey of Manufacturers, webpage*, Washington, DC. Available: *www.census.gov/econ/overview/ma0300.html* [*Accessed 6 June 2007*].

US Census Bureau (2008b), *Foreign Trade Statistics – Advanced Technology Product Definitions*, Washington, DC: *www.census.gov/*. Available: *www.census.gov/* [*Accessed June*].

US Census Bureau (2011), *North American Industry Classification System (NAICS), website*, Washington, DC. Available: *www.census.gov/eos/www/naics/* [*Accessed January*].

US International Trade Administration (2011), *US Aerospace Industry Statistics, website*, Washington, DC. Available: *http://trade.gov/static/doc_aero_stats.asp* [*Accessed 12 February*].

Weiss, S. and A. Amir (1999), *Aerospace Industry*, Encyclopedia Britannica Online, Massachusetts Institute of Technology.

PART I

Chapter 3

Principal Actors in the Space Economy

The space economy includes many different types of public and private actors. This chapter answers the following questions: Who are the key actors involved in space activities and how to obtain information on them? What are the value chains in the space economy?

Actors by organisational structure

There are many different types of actors involved in the space economy and it is often challenging to assess their size and activities. They include: public actors, higher education actors, large industrial groups, but also small and medium enterprises.

Public actors

Governmental bodies play a key role in the space economy as developers, investors, owners, operators, regulators and customers for much of the space infrastructure. As in the case of terrestrial large infrastructure systems (*e.g.* water, energy), government involvement is key to sustaining the overall space economy and to dealing with strategic implications of such complex systems (OECD, 2009).

Space research and development (R&D) in particular is conducted by a myriad of different public actors (*e.g.* space agency, technology centre) and they are not always easily identifiable. The international classification of actors involved in R&D, as described in the *Frascati Manual*, is often used to gather comparable data concerning the R&D activities of governments.

According to the *Frascati Manual* (OECD, 2002), government actors involved in R&D include:

- "All departments, offices and other bodies which furnish, but normally do not sell to the community, those common services, other than higher education, which cannot otherwise be conveniently and economically provided, as well as those that administer the state and the economic and social policy of the community.
- Non-profit institutions (NPIs) controlled and mainly financed by government, but not administered by the higher education sector."
- Public enterprises or partially public enterprises, which are often quite active in the space sector, are included in the "business enterprise" categories.

When looking at other governmental actors involved, particularly as customers for products and services (*e.g.* municipality buying products based on satellite imagery), a classification of these bodies can be used. The government sector's legal entities are usually classified into three categories according to the level of government involved: central and federal government units; provincial and state government units; and local and municipal government units.

Higher education actors (research institutes)

Many universities, laboratories, and research institutions play a key role in space research and development in both OECD and non-OECD countries. They may act as contractors to space agencies and industries, but they constitute a particular source of innovation for the sector (*e.g.* basic research, patenting).

Again according to the *Frascati Manual* definitions, higher education actors include:

- All universities, colleges of technology and other institutions of post-secondary education, whatever their source of finance or legal status.
- It also includes all research institutes, experimental stations and clinics operating under the direct control of or administered by or associated with higher education institutions. The private units of the higher education sector, such as private universities, are included if they are officially recognised by the state.

Business enterprises

Most countries have national statistical business registers, built on administrative and statistical sources (*e.g.* surveys, tax registers). These registers serve as the primary and preferred source of information for business demography statistics (OECD, 2007). One challenge is that the comprehensiveness of these registers varies across countries and time, and the level of detailed information on companies' activities may be limited.

The industrial statistical classifications issue is one major stumbling block when looking for data on enterprises involved in space activities. The industry codes used nationally (as mentioned in Chapter 2) usually give indications about actors involved in the aerospace sector, but even this type of information may be limited. National statistical offices (NSOs) also conduct census on specific sectors from time to time to have a better idea of the businesses involved, but the cost of running a regular census makes this approach unrealistic for most countries with a small aerospace sector.

One other issue relates to the definition of a "space company". Very often enterprises involved in the manufacturing of satellites, launchers or subsystems, and even in space-related services are involved in other economic sectors, and may derive only a small part of their revenues from space activities. An open issue is to decide which revenue threshold a company should reach to be considered a mainly space company. Many industry associations struggle with this problem, and Eurospace has found an elegant methodology when compiling data from its annual survey of the European space industry (Eurospace, 2011). It measures consolidated sales at company level, but also takes into account intermediate sales throughout the value-chain when possible, thus avoiding some possible double-counting. The Canadian Space Agency's survey questionnaire asks companies to report their revenues on two levels, company-wide and space sector's revenues, so it is possible to identify trends over time in growth and downturns directly related to the space sector's activities (CSA, 2011). Concerning NSOs, a few, like the French INSEE for example, integrate specific questions in their aerospace-sector industrial surveys to try and track specifically space-related revenues, so that companies provide a level of detail on their would-be aeronautics, defense and space activities (INSEE, 2009).

As the space economy increasingly includes players that may be included in the ICT sector rather than the aerospace or defense sectors, correctly scoping all the actors is a key issue. Industry mapping could be an important avenue for progress, which would have the objective of better tracking current developers and users of space-related products and services.

Concerning businesses involved in space activities, large aerospace and defense groups tend to be the main actors, many of them being active along entire value chains in space manufacturing and services. Smaller actors are active in specific segments (*e.g.* components, subsystems, equipment, services). Notwithstanding the main mergers of the 1990s and 2000s, an interesting ongoing trend is the emergence of small actors competing in the same market segments as the large groups (*e.g.* OHB in Germany). The small and medium-sized enterprise sector accounts for 99% of firms in the OECD area, and 50%-75% of value added across these countries (OECD, 2010). Although SMEs are quite numerous in services, it is thought that they play a rather small role in space manufacturing. For example in Europe, 77% of space manufacturing employment is thought to be in large groups (Eurospace, 2011). The *Eurostat-OECD Manual on Business Demography Statistics* provides guidelines for the compilation of business demography indicators (OECD, 2007).

Actors by value chain

As noted in OECD (2005), countries with space programmes have generally adopted a broad institutional model for conducting their space-related activities. This generic model involves three general sets of actors: *i)* public agencies that focus on space R&D and science, typically space agencies providing contracts to industry, universities and laboratories; *ii)* public and/or private organisations responsible for the upstream segment of the space industry (*i.e.* spacecraft and launcher manufacturers, providers of launching services); and *iii)* public agencies and/or private actors responsible for the operations of space systems and the development of downstream applications. As noted by the UK Department for Business Innovation and Skills (2010), those actors are part of a long and complex value-added chain comprising two main inter-related sectors:

- The upstream sector includes manufacturers of space hardware and providers of services that enable the launch of systems into space. This comprises prime companies and systems integrators for space and ground equipment, which in turn build on the contributions of subsystem and component suppliers.
- The downstream sector includes operators of satellites and providers of space-enabled products and services. These range from products and services which can only be delivered through space to those which compete with or complement other forms of enabling infrastructures and/or services. Space-related services use a specific satellite capacity, such as bandwidth or imagery, as inputs to provide a more global service to business, government or retail consumers.

Downstream services are as diverse as there are space applications. The services are traditionally divided into three large application domains: telecommunications, Earth observation (also called remote sensing) and navigation. Value chains often involve public agencies as investors and final users. As such, public authorities remain significant customers even in well-established commercial markets, such as telecommunications. In the following example for telecommunications, many companies are active in different segments of the value chain (see Table 3.1).

The value chain starts with the initial R&D, followed by the satellite and launcher systems manufacturing, the actual launch, ensuing satellite management and operations, with the provision of the actual services to the end-customer (*e.g.* broadcast, communications signals). Orders of magnitude in terms of revenues for the diverse actors of the value chain are provided in Table 3.2. The costs of an end-to-end satellite system, based on a commercial geostationary satellite built in North America or Europe (around USD 450 million in total) can be divided as follows between the different main segments:

- Satellite in orbit: 56%.
- Satellite system: 28% (around USD 80-100 million, divided between the system integration tasks 20%, the platform 45%, the payload 35%).
- Launch services: 22%.
- Insurance: 6%.
- Ground segment: 44% (around USD 200 million – user ground segment, mission control centre, satellite control centre) (ITU, 2010).

The same general format (from R&D to service provisioning) applies to other sectors (satellite imagery, navigation and positioning), although with important

Table 3.1. **Actors in satellite telecommunications**

Activity	Description	Selected actors
Satellite operators	A satellite operator finances a satellite's construction and its launch. Each satellite has transponders designed to cover a specific geographic region, or "footprint", thus helping the operator address specific customer markets. The operator then leases transponder capacity to customers, such as service providers, television broadcasters, corporations and governments.	SES, Eutelsat, Intelsat, Inmarsat, Orbcomm, Chinasat Globalstar, Telespazio, Telesat
Ground station equipment providers	The ground equipment, including hubs and Very Small Aperture Terminals (VSATs), is manufactured and supplied by the equipment providers.	MDA, Gilat network Systems, Hugues, iDirect, Thales Alenia Space, AAE Systems Inc., ViaSat, Advantech Satellite Networks, Cerona Networks, Comtech EF Data, NanoTronix, PolarSat, Newtec, ND SatCom, SatPath, Shiron Satellite Communications, STM Group, TSAT, EMS Aviation, International Datacasting Corporation (IDC), SED Systems
Service providers	These are typically either telephony or broadband internet companies who lease capacity from satellite operators, buy equipment from the ground station equipment providers, install and maintain the resulting network and sell full package communication services to the end user.	Spacenet Inc., Spacenet Rural Communications, Stratos Global, Barrett (rural broadband)
Customers	Customers are the organisations and individuals utilising the equipment and satellite communication services. Very large customers, primarily governmental agencies and international companies, sometimes act as their own Service Providers, operating their own ground station equipment. Smaller organizations, including Small & Medium size Enterprises (SME) and Small Offices/Home Offices (SOHOs) work with service providers rather than managing their own infrastructures. Consumers, whether using a telephone, ATM or computer in a rural area might not even know that satellites are providing the network connection.	Governmental agencies, companies active in diverse economic sectors, individual consumers

Source: Adapted from Comsys (2010), Annual VSAT Report, 11th edition, Report prepared by Simon Bull, Comsys, London, January and Gilat (2011), Satellites' Basics, www.gilat.com [Accessed January].

differences in the prevalence of actors involved and in the revenue streams (*e.g.* more governmental agencies as initial R&D funders and final customers).

As the space sector has been spurring more commercial activities outside its traditional science and R&D scope over the years, trying to better identify statistically the different space applications and downstream services has become an important theme. Activities include specific information technology products and services, such as GPS receivers, satellite television

Table 3.2. **An example of the space sector's value chain for satellite telecommunications**

Activity	Description	Selected actors[1]	ISIC Codes	Estimates of EBIT margins[2]
Space systems manufacturing	• Study and design of the mission • Satellite, ground and launch manufacturing • Assembling, integration • Testing • End-to-end systems delivery (satellite, ground, launch service and insurance) • Satellite in-orbit testing • Telemetry, tracking, command and monitoring	Thales Alenia Space, Orbital, Northrop Grunman, OHB technology, EADS, Loral Space & Communications, Lockheed Martin, Ball, RKK Energia	3030	2%-8%
Launch	• Launch system manufacturing • Launch system management (and sale when applicable) • System integration (satellites and launchers)	Lockheed Martin, EADS, RKK Energia, Arianespace, ISRO	3030 5120	1%-6%
Fleet management and operations	• Satellite fleet management and control • Uplink and downlink • Capacity provisioning • End-to-end services	SES, Eutelsat, Intelsat, Inmarsat, Orbcomm, Chinasat Globalstar, Telespazio	6130 6190	30%-40%
Service provisioning	• Service packaging and development • Marketing and sales • Distribution and management of retail channels	Spacenet Inc., Embratel	6190	From negative to 15%

1. Many actors can be active on multiple segments.
2. EBIT: Earnings before interest and taxes (when applicable).
Source: Adapted from Thales Alenia Space (2010).

and even investments in new tourism-related activities (*e.g.* space-related amusement parks, suborbital flights).

Satellite communications have reached maturity in terms of user base. As shown in Table 3.3, users of data networks using satellites (Very small aperture terminal – VSATs) for example include various government departments and agencies, but also banks, insurance companies, general stores, supermarkets, car dealerships, lottery systems, healthcare companies, manufacturers, hotel electrical utilities, oil and gas pipelines, energy production and exploration, timber companies, plantations, maritime shipping fleets to name but a few. This allows a first identification of actual users of space applications, and many market studies focus on this aspect (more indicators of the satellite telecommunications sector are provided in Part 2 of the *Handbook*).

Finally, as already mentioned by OECD (2005), the integration of technologies, thanks to advances in computing power as well as miniaturisation, is both an opportunity and a challenge for developers of space applications. This is also a challenge for trying to statistically map the many new downstream applications. As an example, the markets for broadcasting are undergoing

Table 3.3. **Examples of users of VSAT systems, with system vendors and services operators (2008)**

User	Country	Industry sector	Sites in service	User since	System vendor	Operator
Camelot/GTECH	UK	Lottery	27 000	2007	Hughes	HNS Europe
US Postal Service	US	Post Office	10 400	1998	Gilat	Spacenet
BP/Amoco	US	Gas/Convenience	5 800	1994	Hughes	HNS
Venezuelan Govt Elections	Venezuela	Government	5 000	2004	Gilat	Spacenet RC
Enterprise Rent-a-car	US	Car Rental	4 648	1998	Hughes	Dedicated
National Stock Exchange	India	Financial	3 500	1994	Gilat	Dedicated
Best Western	US	Hospitality	2 383	1995	Hughes	HNS
Shenzhen Securities	China	Financial	2 230	1993	ViaSat	Dedicated
Bombay Stock Exchange	India	Financial	2 000	1997	Hughes	Dedicated
Wendy's Restaurants	US	Restaurant	1 870	2001	Hughes	Hughes
Hollywood Video	US	Retail	1 750	1998	Gilat	Spacenet
Central Bank of Iran	Iran	Banking	1 450	1993	Hughes	ISC
Hungarian State Lottery (SRT)	Hungary	Gaming	1 400	1993	Tridom	GTS
FONCOS	Mexico	Rural	1 100	2005	Hughes	Telmex
Spanish Post Office (OACT)	Spain	Post Office	785	1994	NEC	Telefónica
Shoppers Drug Mart	Canada	Retail	745	1995	ViaSat	Dedicated
Safeway/Argyll	UK	Retail	670	1994	ViaSat	BT
DZ Bank	Germany	Banking	630	2001	Gilat	Satlynx
Farmacias Similares	Mexico	Retail	520	2006	iDirect	Elara
Banco do Brasil	Brazil	Banking	500	1993	Gilat	Embratel

Source: Adapted from Comsys (2010), *Annual VSAT Report, 11th edition*, Report prepared by Simon Bull, Comsys, London, January.

constant change (OECD, 2008). In many countries, the switchover from analogue to digital broadcasting has accelerated, and customers are now able to receive audio-visual content through a number of different networks (satellite, cable, terrestrial, UMTS, IPTV, DVB-H) on a variety of devices (including PCs, mobile telephones and other portable devices). "The convergence of telecommunications and broadcasting, made possible by digitalisation, has resulted in a number of commercial offers of which the triple- (or multiple-) play strategies of telecommunications and cable companies are among the most prominent. This has impacts on how to best determine which technologies are involved."

References

Canadian Space Agency (2011), *State of the Canadian Space Sector 2010, Annual Report*, CSA, Montreal.

Comsys (2010), *Annual VSAT Report, 11th edition*, Report prepared by Simon Bull, Comsys, London, January.

Department for Business Innovation and Skills (2010), "The Space Economy in the UK: An Economic Analysis of the Sector and the Role of Policy", *BIS Ecnomics Paper*, London, February.

Eurospace (2011), *The European Space Industry in 2010, Facts & Figures*, 14th edition, Paris, July.

Gilat (2011), *Satellites' Basics, website*. Available: *www.gilat.com* [*Accessed January*].

INSEE (2009), "L'aéronautique et l'espace en Aquitaine et Midi-Pyrénées, régions d'Aerospace Valley: Résultats de l'enquête 2009", INSEE, Paris, December.

OECD (2002), *Frascati Manual: Proposed Standard Practice for Surveys on Research and Experimental Development*, The Measurement of Scientific and Technological Activities, OECD Publishing, *http://dx.doi.org/10.1787/9789264199040-en*.

OECD (2005), *Space 2030: Tackling Society's Challenges*, OECD Publishing, *http://dx.doi.org/10.1787/9789264008342-en*.

OECD (2007), *OECD Communications Outlook 2007*, OECD Publishing, *http://dx.doi.org/10.1787/comms_outlook-2007-en*.

OECD/Statistical Office of the European Communities, Luxembourg (2008), *Eurostat-OECD Manual on Business Demography Statistics*, OECD Publishing, *http://dx.doi.org/10.1787/9789264041882-en*.

OECD (2009), *Measuring Government Activity*, OECD Publishing, *http://dx.doi.org/10.1787/9789264060784-en*.

OECD (2010), *SMEs, Entrepreneurship and Innovation*, OECD Studies on SMEs and Entrepreneurship, OECD Publishing, *http://dx.doi.org/10.1787/9789264080355-en*.

PART I

Chapter 4

Data Sources and General Methodological Notes

Chapter 4 answers the following questions: Where can I find data on the space sector and the space economy? What methodological caveats should I be aware of?

Economic data sources

A wide diversity of organisations provide economic data on the space sector. They include public organisations (such as space agencies), international organisations (*e.g.* OECD), industry associations, consulting firms and professional associations. The following sections review these existing sources, some less known than others.

Public organisations

There are three main types of public organisations which may be a source of economic data on the space sector: national statistical offices, space agencies and other various governmental bodies.

In most countries, specific governmental agencies – usually National Statistical Offices (NSOs) – have the mandate to publish statistics on the state of the economy. Economic data can be obtained by NSOs via different methods, often through surveys of public organisations and companies, using national industrial classifications to categorise economic activities. However, as seen in Chapter 2, space activities are often embedded in larger aerospace, information and communications technology (ICT) and defense sectors. As a consequence, official data on the space sector tend to lack granularity and are aggregated within much larger industries (Lionnet, 2010). As an alternative, a number of NSOs tend to rely on second-hand data collected by industry associations and/or space agencies, to have a more precise coverage of the industry.

In addition to NSOs, other government departments and space agencies publish official data or contract out to commercial data providers to size up the space industry. But this may bring some methodological issues (scope and definitions, issues with long-time series). The main data coming from these public organisations are published via:

- Annual reports from space agencies or governmental bodies in charge of space activities. In this regard, the Canadian Space Agency has collected space sector data since 1996 via a special industry survey, which has used a consistent set of definitions for the sectors of activity and has focused on ensuring that the Top 30 revenue earners respond to the survey (responses are voluntary but good will built up over the years results in a very high rate of response).
- Specific ad-hoc industry reports (for example in preparation of large events or to review industrial policy).

OECD

There are several OECD databases which may be useful to derive data on the space and aerospace sectors. The primary OECD source is the STAN (or "Structural Analysis") system of databases providing official statistics for industrial and national variables. Other OECD data sources include the Patents database, the UN/OECD International Trade in Commodity Statistics database (ITCS), but also the Annual National Accounts, and selected Exchange Rates and Purchase Power Parities databases (Link to OECD portal: *http://stats.oecd.org/index.aspx*).

The OECD STructural ANalysis (STAN) database provides a comprehensive tool for analysing industrial performance at a relatively detailed level of activity across countries. It includes annual measures of output, labour input, investment and international trade which allow users to construct a wide range of indicators to focus on areas such as productivity growth, competitiveness and general structural change. Through the use of a standard industry list, comparisons can be made across countries. STAN is primarily based on member countries' annual national accounts by activity tables and uses data from other sources, such as national industrial surveys/censuses, to estimate any missing detail. Since many of the data points in STAN are estimated, they do not represent official member country submissions. STAN is based on the International Standard Industrial Classification of all economic activities, (ISIC Rev. 4) and covers all activities (including services).

The STAN Bilateral Trade Database (BTD) is compiled by the Economic Analysis and Statistics Division (EAS) of the Directorate for Science, Technology and Industry (STI). This database is designed to provide analysts with information on exports and imports of goods in OECD countries, broken down by partner country (or geographical area) and by economic activity. BTD is derived from the OECD's International Trade by Commodity Statistics (ITCS) database, where (values and quantities of) imports and exports are compiled according to product classifications and presented by partner country.

The ANBERD (Analytical Business Enterprise Research and Development) database was developed to provide a consistent data set that overcomes the problems of international comparability and breaks in the time series of the official business enterprise R&D data provided to the OECD by its member countries through the OECD's R&D survey. Through the use of established estimation techniques, the OECD Secretariat has created a database for the largest R&D performing countries, as well as a zone total for the European Union. The database is designed to provide analysts with comprehensive and internationally comparable time-series on industrial R&D expenditures.

OECD and Patents Statistics. OECD work on patent statistics is conducted in close co-operation with the members of the Patents Task Force, which brings together the world's major patent offices (European Patent Office, Japanese Patent Office, United States Patent and Trademark Office and the World Intellectual Property Organisation), as well as major providers of statistics and indicators on science and technology (the European Commission, Eurostat, and US National Science Foundation). The main objective is to develop an international statistical infrastructure for patents, with a strong emphasis on the development of databases and methodologies. This infrastructure provides the conditions for improving the comparability and quality of patent indicators, enhancing the accessibility of patent statistics and facilitating the development of a new generation of indicators for policy and research use.

Industry associations

As in any economic sector, diverse industry associations have been established in the space sector at national, regional and international levels. Their aim is to foster industrial co-operation. Some focus on space industry issues (*e.g.* Eurospace) while others cover more largely space, aeronautics and defence (*e.g.* Aerospace Industries Association in the United States). Most of them publish annual figures that are collected via different methodologies (*e.g.* questionnaires to industry and agencies).

Table 4.1. **Industry associations publishing aerospace statistics**

Country/Region	Industry associations	Annual statistics	Website
Australia	Australian Association of Aviation and Aerospace Industries (AAAAI)	No	*www.aaaai.org.au*
Brazil	Associação das Indústrias Aeroespaciais do Brasil (AIAB)	Yes	*www.aiab.com.br*
Canada	Aerospace Industries Association of Canada (AIAC)	Yes	*www.aiac.ca*
Europe	AeroSpace and Defence Industries Association (ASD)	Yes	*www.asd-europe.org*
	Eurospace conducts surveys of the space industry and provides results to ASD	Yes	*www.eurospace.org*
France	Groupement des Industries Françaises Aéronautiques et Spatiales (GIFAS)	Yes	*www.gifas.asso.fr*
Germany	German Aerospace Industries Association (BDLI)	Yes	*www.bdli.de*
India	Society of Indian Aerospace Technologies and Industries (SIATI)	No	*www.siati.in*
Italy	Associazione delle Industrie per l'Aerospazio i Sistemi e la Difesa (AIAD)	Yes	*www.aiad.it*
Japan	Japanese Aerospace Industries Association (SJAC),	Yes	*www.sjac.or.jp*
Spain	ProEspacio is the association of Spanish space companies	Yes	*www.proespacio.org*
United Kingdom	United Kingdom Aerospace, Defence and Security Group	Yes	*www.adsgroup.org.uk*
United States	Aerospace Industries Association (AIA)	Yes	*www.aia-aerospace.org*

Consulting firms

In addition to industry associations, many specialised consulting firms provide their services to the actors of the space sector (*e.g.* Euroconsult, Futron, Northern Sky Research, The Tauri Group). They publish and sell annual reports on the state of the sector and/or market studies on specific segments of the industry (*e.g.* telecommunications, Earth observation).

Over the years, generalist consulting firms have also developed dedicated expertise in the space sector to address a growing industry and rising government demand for market studies and independent assessments (*e.g.* RAND Corporation, PriceWaterHouse, Frost&Sullivan, Booz Allen Hamilton, and Deloitte).

Although background economic data for these commercial studies are understandably proprietary, the recurring lack of basic methodological notes attached to the data (*i.e.* inflation taken into account or not, real or nominal exchange rates, etc.) is a significant drawback in some cases.

Professional associations

The number of professional and scientific associations involved in space activities has grown over the years. Their activities tend mainly to cover engineering and scientific issues, although over the last decade, other governance and space economics-related aspects have been addressed in conferences and workshops (*e.g.* economic sessions in the framework of the International Astronautical Federation).

Many of these associations hold space-related conferences and congresses (*e.g.* Association Aéronautique et Astronautique de France [AAAF], American Institute of Aeronautics And Astronautics [AIAA], International Astronautical Federation [IAF], National Academy of Sciences, Space Studies Board. and the International Academy of Astronautics [IAA]).

Non-profit associations have also developed, particularly in the United States (*e.g.* The Planetary Society, the Space Foundation, the Space Frontier, the National Space Society). In co-operation with consulting firms, they develop position papers and more extensive reports on the space sector, such as the Space Foundation's annual *Space Report*, which collects economic data from a large range of sources (The Space Foundation, 2010).

Media sources

A final category of data sources concerns the media, particularly specialised magazines. A number of media sources publish special annual editions with trends on space industry contracts and overall markets (*e.g.* Space News, Aviation and Space Week, Air et Cosmos).

Table 4.2. **Selected sources of data on the space sector (2010-11)**

	Official data	Industry associations and other private sources
Brazil	• Brazilian Space Agency (2011)	• Brazilian Aerospace Industries Association (2011)
Canada	• Canadian Space Agency (2011) • Treasury Board of Canada (2011)	• Aerospace Industries Association of Canada (2011)
Europe	• European Space Agency (2010)	• Eurospace (2011)
France	• Centre National d'Etudes Spatiales (2010) • INSEE (2009) (2010a) (2010b) • Direction générale des douanes et droits indirects (2010)	• GIFAS (2010)
India	• Indian Space Research Organisation (2010)	–
Italy	• Italian Space Agency (2010) • National Italian Institute of Statistics (2010)	• Associazione delle Industrie per l'Aerospazio i Sistemi e la Difesa (AIAD)
Norway	• Norwegian Space Centre (2010a) (2010b)	–
Spain	• Instituto Nacional de Técnica Aeroespacial (INTA) (2011)	• ProEspacio (2011)
UK	• Department for Business Innovation and Skills (2010) • UK Space Agency (2010a) (2010b)	• UK Aerospace Defence and Security Group (2011) • Oxford Economics (2009)
US	• NASA (2010) • US Census Bureau (2010) • US Department of Labor (2010) • National Science Foundation (2010)	• Aerospace Industry Association (2011) • Satellite Industry Association (2010) • The Space Foundation (2010)

Note: The references for the reports appear at the end of the chapter.

The data for these annual reports may be based on questionnaires sent to the industry and/or on public information available on company's website. Methodologies may vary over time (*e.g.* inflation taken into account in companies revenues' reporting), and the number of respondents may change in the case of surveys.

Methodological notes on economic data

Whenever collecting, producing, or using economic data on the space sector, one should be aware of some basic methodological constraints which may affect the quality of the data. The following points have been addressed within the OECD Space Forum (OECD, 2007). They may be applicable to several types of indicators.

What is an indicator?

An indicator is a quantifiable measurement (*e.g.* a number, a ratio) that can show changes and trends over time. Indicators are powerful tools that serve many purposes, as instruments for performance evaluation and public information. When developing indicators, key challenges include 1) making data comparable when different sources of information are taken into account, and 2) making data comparable over time, using established methodologies that may be revised over time. Via national and international co-operation, OECD has already established common approaches and frameworks for developing, measuring and using hundreds of indicators on various sectors of the economy, indicators which are updated on a rolling basis, as data become available.

Exploring indicators on the space economy aims in the long run to provide better awareness of the space sector and its related potential impacts. At the international level, attempts have been made in the past (in 1994 and again in 2002) to align resources to accomplish better space-related data comparability, but without much success(Hertzfeld, 2003). One objective of the current exercise via the OECD Space Forum is to discuss, compare and promote practices that may be used by national statistical offices (NSOs) and other actors, in both the public and private sectors, to attain an improved level of harmonisation and international data comparability over time.

Examining production data and sales

Production represents the value of goods and/or services produced in a year, whether sold or stocked. The related measure "turnover" corresponds to the actual sales in the year and can be greater than production in a given year if all production is sold together with stocks from previous years. While production and turnover will be different in any given year, their averages over a long period of time should converge. Some care should be taken with the interpretation of production because it includes intermediate inputs (such as energy, materials and services required to produce final output, see Section below on double counting). Any output of intermediate goods consumed within the same sector is also recorded as output, with the impact of such intra-sector flows depending on the coverage of the sector. For this reason, value added is often considered a better measure of output.

Double counting

Double counting error, whereby an item is taken into account more than once, is a frequent problem particularly with statistics in the commercial space sector.

This is a particular concern when looking at production data. Production represents the value of goods and services produced by an entity. However, if one enterprise produces an item for USD 100, which is then sold to another enterprise in the same industry that produces USD 500 of goods, there is a need to identify the USD 100 item separately when analysing the global value created or run the risk of "double counting". The USD 100 component will appear in the production value of both the originating manufacturer and the company including that component into its product. One way to avoid this is to use value added which may not always be as easily readable or accurate, but will exclude the USD 100 component in measuring the output of the enterprise purchasing it from the original manufacturer.

Similar problems may also exist when examining other variables such as sales. Adding-up sales from companies present throughout the value chain (company A selling to company B selling to company C – total revenues of the value chain do not equal automatically revenues A + B + C), lead to an overestimation of revenues derived from commercial activities.

Current and constant values

Choosing to use current or constant values is an important issue, when presenting economic data. This may affect the message given by the figures.

Current values. Current values (or values in nominal terms) represent the amount at that period of time when it was originally expensed or budgeted. The value is not adjusted for the effects of inflation or other price changes.

Constant values. Constant values (or values in real terms) indicate what an amount would be worth in comparison to some value from a base period. This is done mainly to eliminate price differences from year to year and ease comparisons. The most common way is to use an index, usually the Consumer Price Index (CPI), to convert the values into that of the base year. CPI is a measure that examines how the price of a weighted-basket of goods and services purchased in the basic economy varies over time.

Limitations with constant values and space. A particular problem in trying to put the space sector's values into constant dollars is determining which index to use when trying to put values into a base year for space products or services. CPI measures changes in the value of goods and services in the general economy, but so far no price indices exist that specifically relate to space items. The prices of space items may vary considerably from year to year due to a number of factors: different specifications, varying countries, dual use *versus* single usage and other issues.

Example. The government of a country has R&D expenditures of USD 100 in 2010 and 2011. The current value would be USD 100 in both years, regardless of the inflation rate, as that was the actual amount of expenditure for those respective years. With constant prices, the value spent in 2010 (the base year) would be USD 100. In the next year, 2011, and assuming an inflation rate of 10%, the original USD 100 expenditures would be worth only USD 90 (100/[1 + r]), where r is the inflation rate. The USD 10 reduction in 2011 constant values indicate that USD 100 in 2011 would only be able to buy USD 90 worth of items from 2010.

Where to find deflators? Whenever possible, industry-specific price deflators should be used, however deflators are typically not available for detailed industry categories and using existing country-specific deflators limits cross-country comparison (OECD, 2011). OECD Consumer and Producer Prices datasets can be used for the 34 OECD member countries and for some six non-member countries: Brazil, China, India, Indonesia, Russian Federation and South Africa. They are subsets of the Main Economic Indicators (MEI) database, which contains a wide variety economic statistics (*http://stats.oecd.org/mei/*). For a global coverage, data from the World Bank can be used (*http://data.worldbank.org/indicator*).

Nominal and real exchange rates

Exchange rates indicate the value of one currency in terms of another. One of the most common methods is to provide the exchange rates as they are, without adjusting them for the price differences that may exist between the countries involved; these are known as nominal exchange rates.

When using this type of exchange rate to compare government space budgets, the differences in currencies may impair comparability considerably. Countries with strong currencies may see their budget over-valued, while others may be undervalued despite large space programmes (*e.g.* India, Russian Federation).

To remedy this distortion, real exchange rates try to ensure their currencies reflect differences in price levels, so as to reflect more appropriately what a good or service in one country may trade for in another. One of the most popular ways to try to estimate the real exchange rate is to use purchasing power parities (PPP).

Purchasing power parity (PPP)

Comparing economies. In the early 1980s, the OECD and Eurostat established a programme to provide internationally comparable price and volume measures of GDP and its component expenditures for the EU member states and the OECD member countries. This programme has since been enlarged with more than 40 countries contributing data. Before purchasing power parities (PPPs) became available, exchange rates had to be used to make international comparisons.

But exchange rates do not reflect the relative purchasing powers of currencies in their national markets. Exchange rate converted data are generally misleading on the relative sizes of economies, overstating the size of economies with relatively high price levels and understating the size of economies with relatively low price levels. There is an additional problem that they are often subject to violent fluctuations. This means that countries may suddenly appear to become "richer" or "poorer", even though in reality there has been little or no change in the relative volume of goods and services produced. Averaging exchange rates over several years dampens their fluctuations, but does not bring them closer to PPPs.

How do PPPs work? If the PPP for GDP between France and the United States is 0.97 euros to the dollar, it can be inferred that for every dollar spent on the GDP in the United States, 0.97 euros would have to be spent in France to purchase the same volume of goods and services. Purchasing the "same volume of goods and services" does not mean that identical baskets of goods and services will be purchased in both countries. The composition of the baskets will vary between countries and reflect differences in tastes, cultures, climates, income levels, price structures and product availability, but both baskets will, in principle, provide equivalent satisfaction or utility.

Limitations. PPPs are statistical constructs rather than precise measures. While they provide the best available estimate of the size of each country's economy and of the economic well-being of the country in relation to the others in the comparison, they are, like all statistics, point estimates lying within a range of estimates – the "error margin" – that includes the true value. PPPs are also an aggregate economic measure. Therefore, lower level economic comparisons using PPPs are not always recommended, although they provide useful orders of magnitude. Cross-country productivity comparisons by industry, for example, should not be undertaken unless industry-specific PPPs are available.

Where to find PPPs? The OECD makes available purchasing power parities data on its website (*http://stats.oecd.org/index.aspx*), as well as the World Bank (*http://data.worldbank.org/indicator*).

Productivity

Productivity is a measure of efficiency and represents the amount of output that is derived from a given amount of input. Productivity can be measured in physical (*e.g.* total number of units produced per unit of input) or financial (*e.g.* the US dollar value of outputs per unit of input) terms. One of the most commonly used types is labour productivity, which measures the value of output provided for a given unit of labour (*e.g.* usually measured in terms of either per worker or per labour-hour). However in high-tech industries, such as the space manufacturing industry, much of the increase in labour productivity may be just as attributable to newer technologies (*i.e.* machines) or better management practices, as to a better trained and educated workforce.

References

Aerospace Industries Association of Canada (2011), *AIAC Guide to Canada's Aerospace Industry 2010-2011*, Ottawa.

AIA (Aerospace Industry Association) (2011), *US Aerospace Statistics, website*, Washington, DC. Available: *www.aia-aerospace.org/economics/aerospace_statistics/* [*Accessed 10 March*].

Associação das Indústrias Aeroespaciais do Brasil (AIAB) (2011), *Números da Associação das Indústrias Aeroespaciais do Brasil*, EAB, Brasilia, Brazil, *www.aiab.org.br*.

Brazilian Space Agency (2011), *Annual Report*, EAB, Brasilia, Brazil, *www.aeb.gov.br*.

Canadian Space Agency (2011), *State of the Canadian Space Sector 2010*, Annual Report, CSA, Montreal.

CNES (Centre National d'Études Spatiales) (2010), *Rapport d'activité 2009*, Paris.

Department for Business Innovation and Skills (2010), "The Space Economy in the UK: An Economic Analysis of the Sector and the Role of Policy", *BIS Economics Paper*, London, February.

Direction générale des douanes et droits indirects (2010), "Le chiffre du commerce extérieur", *Études et éclairages* n° 15, Département des statistiques et des études économiques, Juillet.

European Space Agency (2010), *Annual Report*, ESA, paris.

Eurospace (2011), *The European Space Industry in 2010, Facts & Figures*, 14th edition, Paris, July.

GIFAS (2010), *Annual Report 2008-2009*, Groupement des industries Françaises Aéronautiques et Spatiales (GIIFAS), Paris, July.

Hertzfeld, H. (2003), *Space Economic Data*, Report prepared for the US Department of Commerce, Office of Space Commercialization, Space Policy Institute, Washington, DC.

ISRO (Indian Space Research Organization) (2010), *Annual Report 2009-2010*, ISRO, Bangalore.

INSEE (2009), *L'aéronautique et l'espace en Aquitaine et Midi-Pyrénées,* régions d'Aerospace Valley : Résultats de l'enquête 2009, INSEE, Paris, December.

INSEE (2010a), "Début 2010, l'aéronautique encore au ralenti, le spatial accélère", *Aquitaine e-publications*, INSEE, Paris, July.

INSEE (2010b), *Indices de chiffre d'affaires dans le commerce, les services et les transports, Transports aériens de fret et transports spatiaux*, Données mensuelles, Paris, Database accessed 11 July.

Instituto Nacional de Técnica Aeroespacial (INTA) (2011), *Memoria del INTA 2010 – INTA 2010 Annual Report*, Madrid.

(ASI) Italian Space Agency (2010), *Strategic Plan 2010-2020*, Rome, December.

Lionnet, P. (2010), "Methodological issues and hurdles with space economic data", *61st International Astronautical Congress*, Prague, CZ.

NASA (2010), *NASA FY 2010 Performance and Accountability Report*, NASA, Washington, DC, United States, November.

National Italian Institute of Statistics (2010), *Technological Sectors Database*, Istat, Rome, *www.istat.it*.

National Science Foundation (2010), *Science and Engineering Indicators 2010*, Washington, DC.

Norwegian Space Centre (2010a), *Norges langtidsplan for romvirksomhet Handlingsplan*, 2010-2013, Oslo, June (in Norwegian).

Norwegian Space Centre (2010b), *Norsk industri og-ESA deltakelse: Evaluering av industrielle ringvirkninger av Norsk deltakelse I ESAsamarbeidet*, Oslo, March (in Norwegian).

OECD (2007), *The Space Economy at A Glance 2007*, OECD Publishing, *http://dx.doi.org/10.1787/9789264040847-en*.

OECD (2011), *OECD Guide to Measuring the Information Society 2011*, OECD Publishing, *http://dx.doi.org/10.1787/9789264113541-en*.

Oxford Economics (2009), *The Case for Space: The Impact of Space Derived Services and Data*, Commissioned by South East England Development Agency (SEEDA), London, UK, July.

ProEspacio (2011), Informe anual – *La evolucioñ del sector espacial español*, Madrid, Spain.

Satellite Industry Association (2010), *State of the Satellite Industry Report*, Report prepared by Futron Corp., Washington, DC, June.

The Space Foundation (2010), *The Space Report*, Colorado Springs, CO.

Treasury Board of Canada (2011), *Reports on Plans and Priorities (RPP): The Canadian Space Agency 2010-11*, CSA, Ottawa.

UK Aerospace Defence and Security Group (2011), *UK Aerospace Industry Survey 2011*, London.

UK Space Agency (2010a), *The Size and Health of the UK Space Industry*, Swindon, Wiltshire, November.

UK Space Agency (2010b), *UK in space 2010*, Annual report, Swindon, Wiltshire.

US Census Bureau (2010), *2009 Annual Survey of Manufactures*, Statistics for Industry Groups and Industries, Washington, DC.

US Department of Labor (2010), *Career Guide to Industries: Aerospace Product and Parts Manufacturing*, Washington, DC: Bureau of Labor Statistics. Available: *www.bls.gov/oco/cg/* [*Accessed March 10, 2010*].

PART II

Overview of Indicators for the Space Economy

PART II

Chapter 5

Readiness Indicators: Inputs to the Space Economy

Chapter 5 examines the readiness factors of the space economy, i.e. different elements that are necessary for the development of space activities. These elements encompass the technical, financial and social infrastructures that enable the production of space-related hardware or the provision of services. This chapter examines the following indicators: government budgets for space activities (both for public space programmes and for R&D activities) and human capital.

Governmental budgets for space activities

National and other institutional budgets often contribute to the start-up and development of capital-intensive and high-technology sectors such as space. This section provides details on two aspects of government budgets dedicated to space activities: 1) civilian space programmes as presented annually in Government Budget Appropriations or Outlays for Research and Development (GBAORD); and 2) public institutional space budgets, covering both civilian and military budgets.

Government Budget Appropriations or Outlays for R&D (GBAORD) in civilian space programmes

Government R&D appropriations or outlays on R&D (GBAORD) data are assembled by national authorities analysing their budget for R&D content and classifying these outlays by "socio-economic objective" on the basis of the NABS 2007 (Nomenclature for the analysis and comparison of scientific programmes and budgets), (OECD, 2002). The data provided in the OECD database for GBAORD cover the period 1981-2011 (updated annually in February).

GBAORD data have the advantage of being timely and reflecting current government priorities. However, the data refer to budget provisions, not to actual expenditures, and the breakdown in socio-economic objectives brings some limitations (*i.e.* the "exploration and exploitation of space" category excludes military space programmes, which are included in a specific "defense" category). GBAORD data can provide trends, which can be usefully complemented by other data (*e.g.* institutional budgets).

The OECD recommends indices based on constant Purchasing Power Parities (PPPs) for the analysis of relative growth performance between countries and over time. Current PPPs allow useful snapshots for a given year. It is important to remember that PPPS are statistical constructs rather than precise measures, so differences between countries should be interpreted with caution (see previous chapter for more information on how to use PPPs).

When analysing GBAORD data, comparability may be affected by the fact that GBAORD tends to represent expenditures of the federal or central government only. The OECD *Frascati Manual*, which provides useful guidelines for R&D comparisons, does suggest the inclusion of provincial/state data if they are "significant" (OECD, 2002). Thus, comparability may be limited to the extent that data compilers perceive expenditures of other levels of government as significant. Also, several countries with large space programmes are usually not included, due to current lack of GBAORD data (*e.g.* Brazil, China, and India).

Figure 5.1. **Civil space programmes as a percentage of civil GBAORD for selected countries**

1981-2010 (or latest available year)

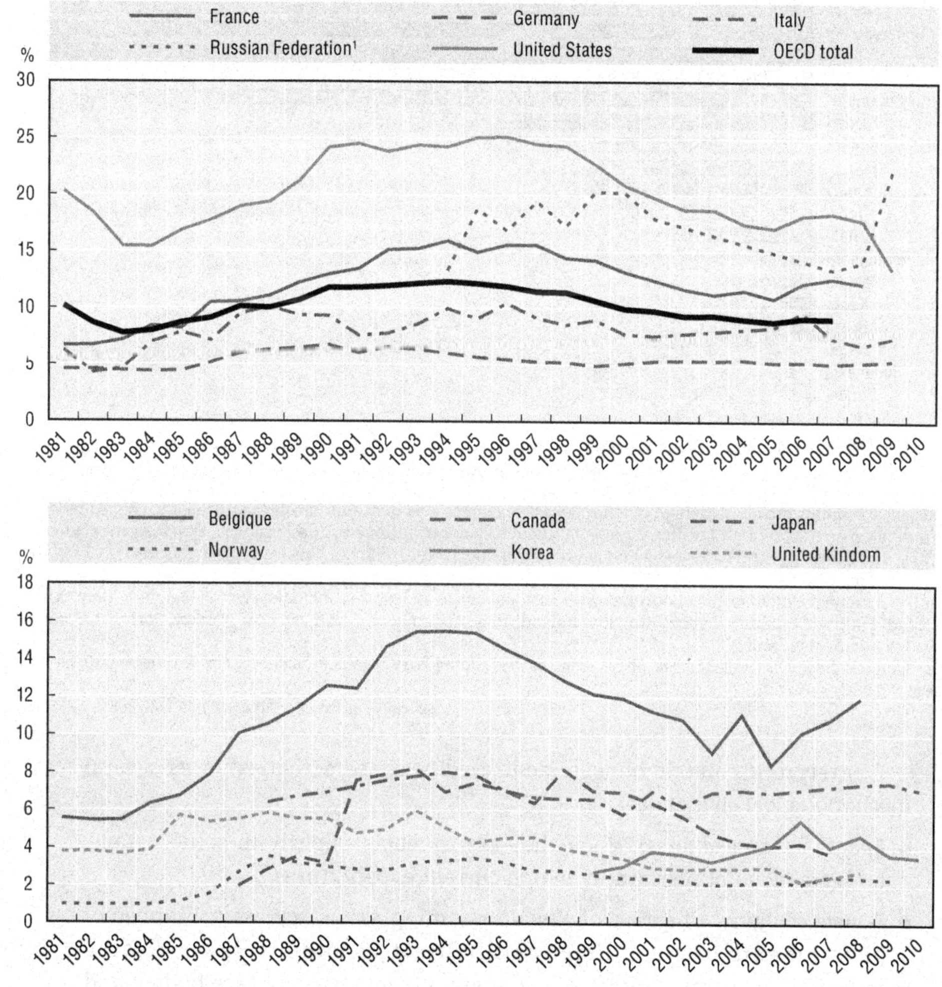

1. Non-OECD country.

Source: OECD, *Main Science and Technology Indicators database*, August 2010.

StatLink http://dx.doi.org/10.1787/888932576776

National budgets for space

Space budgets refer to the amounts that governments provide to public sector agencies or organisations to achieve space-related goals (*e.g.* better communications, security). Space budgets often serve both civilian and military objectives. In *The Space Economy at a Glance 2011*, data are derived from institutional sources and provide conservative estimates (OECD, 2011b).

Figure 5.2. **Conservative estimates of space budgets of G20 countries, 2010**

Current USD million

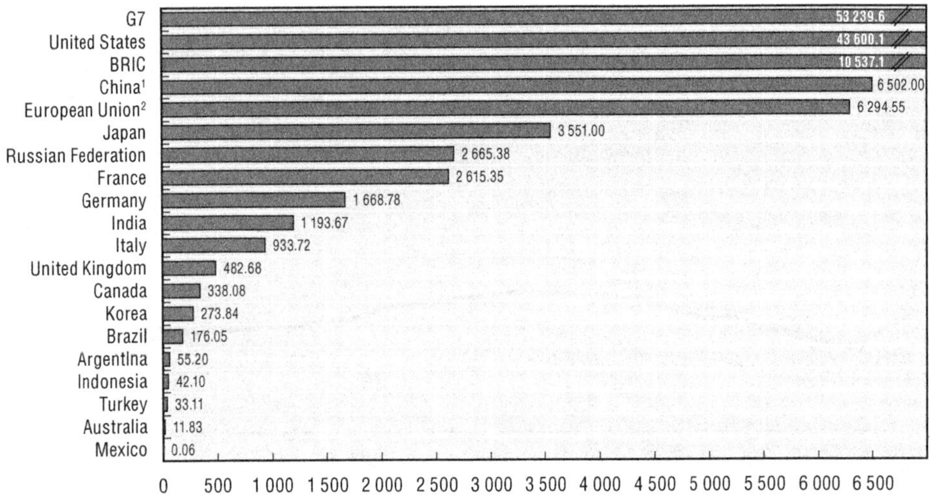

Note: These estimates provide orders of magnitude, as exchange rates may alter direct comparability. Figures reflect all space investments (civil and military budgets) including contributions to the European Space Agency where applicable. Data missing for Saudi Arabia and South Africa. BRIC refers to Brazil, Russia, India and China.

1. Unofficial data.
2. For the European Union, only 17 countries with national space budgets are included Austria, Belgium, Denmark, Finland, France, Germany, Greece, Hungary, Ireland, Italy, Luxembourg, Netherlands, Norway, Portugal, Spain, Sweden and Switzerland.

Source: Adapted from OECD (2011), *The Space Economy at a Glance 2011*, OECD Publishing, *http://dx.doi.org/10.1787/9789264111790-en*, p. 25.

StatLink http://dx.doi.org/10.1787/888932576605

Interpreting public budgets dedicated to space activities poses several methodological challenges:

- *Budget vs. expenditures*: When they are available publicly in some details, budgets may not necessarily match current expenditures.
- *Double counting:* The risk of double counting exists too, as a number of governments provide direct and indirect funding to space-related international organizations, *e.g.* adding up France's total space budget and the budgets from the European Space Agency (which already includes France's contribution).

- *Limited data availability:*
  - Countries with very small space offices or activities often do not publish detailed budget breakdown.
  - Significant portions of military-related space budgets may not be published because of secrecy and/or may be classified under other areas of government expenditure.
  - Moreover, some civilian space-related budget lines may be classified under other areas of government expenditure, *e.g.* telecommunications or R&D, and not under "space".
- *Budgets for different space disciplines:* Although aggregate data for public budgets in science can be found for many countries, as shown in the *OECD Main Science and Technology Indicators*, very often the budgets for different scientific disciplines are not available in detail and are not comparable over time. In the case of astronomy for example, after reviewing the state of information available today on OECD countries' funding of astronomy and space sciences, it appears that there are relatively few data available that are internationally comparable (based on space agencies' and scientific groups' data) (Seth *et al.*, 2009). Even on national basis, discrepancies can be quite important (National Research Council, 2010).
- *Comparability issues:*
  - Differences in budget line definitions across countries: budgets are usually organised in different categories (science, applicative areas), according to national definitions, making data difficult to compare directly.
  - The start of the fiscal year and budget appropriation differs from country to country (*e.g.* Japan, United States, France), so that annual data are not always readily comparable.
  - Currencies and PPPs affect international comparability (see previous chapter). Expenditures in what are currently lower income countries such as China and India may have a higher purchasing power than similar expenditures in high-income countries, because the costs of labour and services are lower. The real, *i.e.* PPP-adjusted, expenditure in such countries may therefore be higher than that indicated by a comparison based solely on exchange rates.
- *Defence sector issues:* The importance of military space budgets should not be underestimated. Military budgets, dedicated to R&D programmes (*e.g.* missiles, navigation systems) or to operational programmes (*e.g.* "spy" satellites, ground-based stations for communications), represent for some countries a large part of their space investments. Space programmes are often dual use in nature, meaning the capability they provide can be used

for both civilian and military objectives. Governments may therefore fund space programmes as civilian endeavors while in fact part of the R&D is dedicated to military objectives. A *contrario*, many governments include most or a large part of the space investments in their defence budgets (China, United States). This raises issues in evaluating those budgets. The type of weapons system that should or should not be included in an overall estimate of military space programme is also not clear. For instance, should strategic ballistic missiles be included *de facto* in space programmes, if the budget information is available? The RAND Corporation measured the US federal spending within the aerospace industry from 1993 to 2003 (Hogan *et al.*, 2005). The study provides a detailed examination of the Federal Procurement Data System (FPDS), with the specific purpose of tracking all government aerospace procurement and R&D expenditures from 1993 to 2003. The results only approximate overall spending because they do not include classified military programmes, which could not be identified using the Federal Procurement Data System.

Human resources

Human capital is key to the development and sustainability of the space sector. The sector is home to highly skilled professionals (*i.e.* technicians, scientists and engineers). Existing data on space-related human capital are very fragmented. Official employment statistics on the sector are poor, lacking in both quality and detail. To some extent, the gaps can be filled by non-official statistics, mainly from industry associations, and usually focus on the space manufacturing industry while the larger services sector is often ignored.

The *Manual on the Measurement of Human Resources* or *Canberra Manual* was developed in the 1990s to provide a statistical framework for compiling data on stocks and flows of human resources in science and technology (HRST) detailing seven broad fields: natural sciences, engineering and technology, medical sciences, agricultural sciences, social sciences, humanities, and other fields (OECD, 1995). HRST are people engaged in, or who have the relevant training to be engaged in, the production, development, diffusion, application and maintenance of systematic scientific and technological (S&T) knowledge. HRST are defined by the *Canberra Manual* as people who fulfil one or other of the following conditions:

- Successfully completed education at the tertiary level in an S&T field of study (*i.e.* HRSTE).
- Not formally qualified as above, but employed in an S&T occupation where the above qualifications are normally required (*i.e.* HRSTO).

There are two harmonised standards which give definitions for education and occupations internationally: the International Standard Classification of

Education (ISCED) which provides levels of formal educational achievements and the International Standard Classification of Occupation (ISCO) detailing the type of occupation. Despite efforts to harmonise statistical information on education and employment at the international level, current data sets can still lead to conflicting interpretations (OECD, 2011a).

By way of illustration, data about the UK space workforce are examined below. The data come from two sources, using differing scope and methodologies. The figure below on space manufacturing employment uses data from the Eurospace Industry Association's annual survey. Over six years, the UK space sector employment, *i.e.* the space manufacturing sector, has ranged between 3 200 and 3 580 Full Time Equivalents.

Figure 5.3. **Space manufacturing employment in the UK (2003-08)**

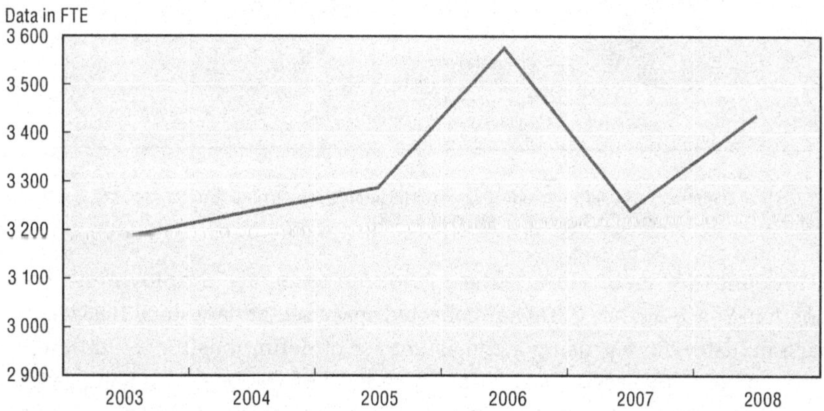

Source: Eurospace (2009), *The European Space Industry in 2008, Facts & Figures*, 12th edition, Paris.

The second source for UK space employment is the study conducted by Oxford Economics, which relied on 2006-07 data collected through surveys of the British National Space Centre (BNSC) and other consulting firms (Oxford Economics, 2009). The survey finds that in 2006-07, some 19 100 people were employed in space-related manufacturing and services jobs in the United Kingdom. The upstream space industry employs around 5 850 workers (up from just over 4 700 in 1999). Of these around 2 500 were in space prime companies, 1 200 in the subsystems suppliers, and 300 in the component or material suppliers. The downstream space industry employed around 13 250 workers. Of these around 9 700 people worked for satellite broadcast service providers and around 1 500 for satellite communication service providers. Support products and services employed almost 1 000 people, whereas earth observation and user equipment suppliers employed around 500 people each.

Figure 5.4. **Direct employment in upstream and downstream segments in the UK space industry**

(2006-07)

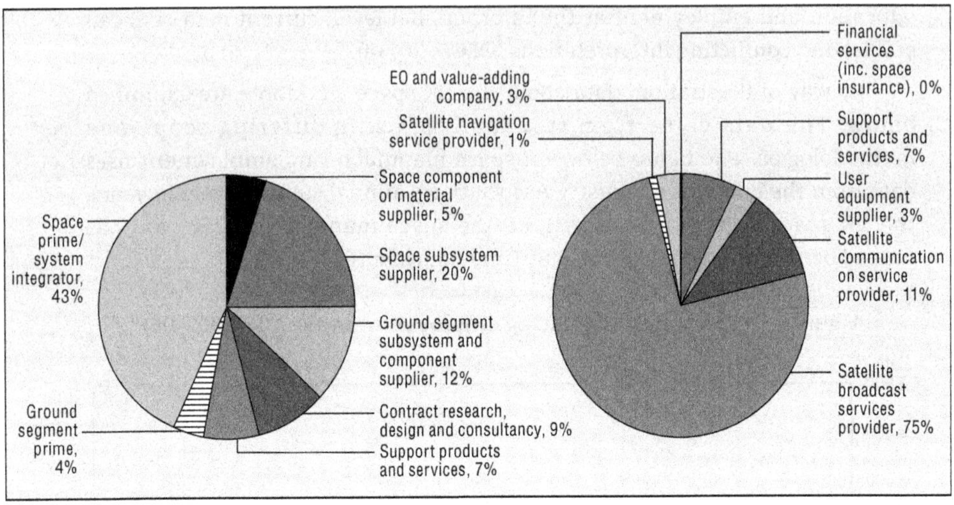

Note: Total: 19 100 people.

Source: BNSC/Oxford Economics (2009), *The Case for Space: The Impact of Space Derived Services and Data*, Commissioned by South East England Development Agency (SEEDA), London, UK.

As another example of existing source for space employment, the Canadian Space Agency (CSA) has collected space sector data since 1996 via its space industry survey, using a consistent set of definitions for the different sectors of activity. Based on its rather high level of responses over the years, CSA can provide breakdowns by type of position (technical vs. sales), region of the country, as well as by sector of activity (*e.g.* telecommunications vs. navigation) (CSA, 2011).

It remains that a number of key issues for the space sector include:

- *Sectors of activity:* Statistics on space activities are usually embedded in larger aerospace and defence categories, making it difficult to separate the different activities. Statistics on defence personnel are especially challenging to obtain, particularly in non-OECD countries. In the space sector itself, different specific subsectors co-exist (*e.g.* telecommunications, earth observation) with the added need to identify complex value chains.
- *Counting time or people?* Countries and industry associations may report employment in Full-Time Equivalents (FTEs) (counting shifts, not individuals) or numbers of persons employed. This is important to take into account when trying to compare data.
- *Data sources:* Official employment statistics on the space sector, when they exist, are often lacking in quality and detail. To some extent, the gaps can be

filled by non-official statistics, mainly from industry associations, which often focus on the larger aerospace sector – sometimes with a category on space manufacturing industry, but more often than not, occulting the larger services sector (*e.g.* professionals in satellite telecommunications). Increasingly private one-off surveys from consulting firms try to cover the larger field of space applications.

Based on this, one important aspect when collecting data on human resources is to characterise clearly the scope of the survey (*i.e.* identifying the segments of the value chain to be covered), and to define the categories of jobs to be surveyed.

References

Canadian Space Agency (2011), *State of the Canadian Space Sector 2010, Annual Report*, CSA, Montreal.

Eurospace (2009), *The European Space Industry in 2008, Facts & Figures*, 12th edition, Paris.

Hogan, T., D. Fossum, D.J. Johnson and L.S. Painter (2005), *Scoping Aerospace: Tracking Federal Procurement and R&D Spending in the Aerospace Sector*, RAND Corp. Prepared for the Office of the Secretary of Defense, Santa Monica, CA.

National Research Council (2010), *New Worlds, New Horizons in Astronomy and Astrophysics*, Space Studies Board, Aeronautics and Space Engineering Board, Washington, DC.

OECD/Statistical Office of the European Communities, Luxembourg (1995), *Measurement of Scientific and Technological Activities: Manual on the Measurement of Human Resources Devoted to S&T – Canberra Manual*, OECD Publishing, *http://dx.doi.org/10.1787/9789264065581-en*.

OECD (2002), *Frascati Manual: Proposed Standard Practice for Surveys on Research and Experimental Development*, The Measurement of Scientific and Technological Activities, OECD Publishing, *http://dx.doi.org/10.1787/9789264199040-en*.

OECD (2011a), *Skills for Innovation and Research*, OECD Publishing, *http://dx.doi.org/10.1787/9789264097490-en*.

OECD (2011b), *The Space Economy at A Glance 2011*, OECD Publishing, *http://dx.doi.org/10.1787/9789264111790-en*.

Oxford Economics (2009), *The Case for Space: The Impact of Space Derived Services and Data*, Commissioned by South East England Development Agency (SEEDA), London, UK.

Seth, A. *et al.* (2009), *Employment & Funding in Astronomy, Astro2010: The Astronomy and Astrophysics Decadal Survey*, Position Papers.

PART II

Chapter 6

Intensity Indicators: Selected Activities and Outputs in the Space Economy

The intensity indicators of the space economy are constituted by all the diverse outputs (products, services, science) that are produced or provided by the space sector. These outputs are very diverse in nature, from commercial revenues from industry, scientific productivity such as patents, to number of space missions or space launches. This chapter examines methodological issues specific to a few selected intensity indicators: space manufacturing, space-based applications, international trade in space products, and space-related patents.

The manufacturing space industry

The manufacturing space industry is the industrial activity for which there are the most data available, but there are still clear methodological limitations when trying to make international comparisons.

As mentioned in previous chapters, the current edition of the United Nations International Standard Industrial Classification (ISIC Rev. 4) includes most parts of the space sector under different aggregate categories. There is no specific "space industry" classification in ISIC, and disentangling official space sector statistics from the larger aerospace and defence sectors remains a challenge in most countries. Interestingly enough, this is not the case for Chinese official data, as China has its own statistical classifications system separating space and aeronautical activities. Other methodological issues arise though, as the funding of the Chinese space industry lacks some transparency.

The next three figures provide examples of data available from the European, Japanese and Chinese space manufacturing sectors (note all data are in national currencies).

Figure 6.1. **Consolidated sales and employment by European space companies, 2000-09**

Billions of constant euros and FTE

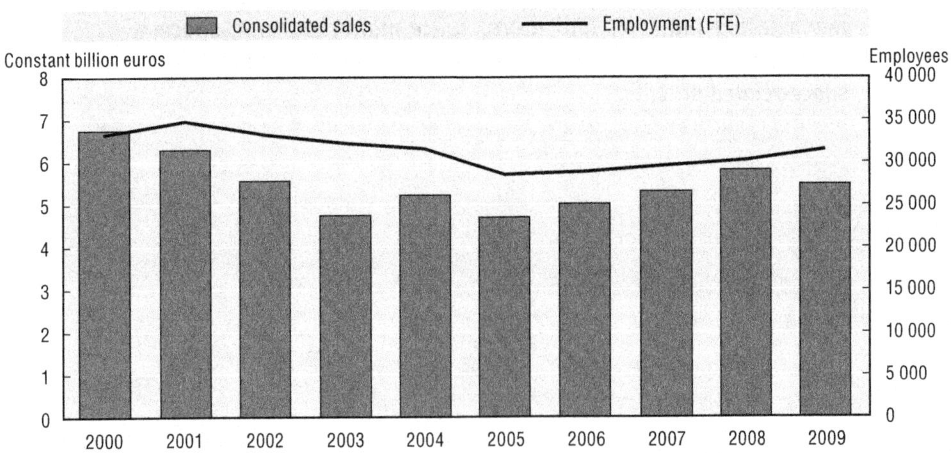

Source: Eurospace, 2010 in OECD (2011), *The Space Economy at a Glance 2011*, OECD Publishing, *http://dx.doi.org/10.1787/9789264111790-en*, p. 61.

StatLink http://dx.doi.org/10.1787/888932576624

Figure 6.2. **Consolidated sales and employment by Japanese space manufacturing companies, 2000-11**

Billions of Japanese yen and number of workers

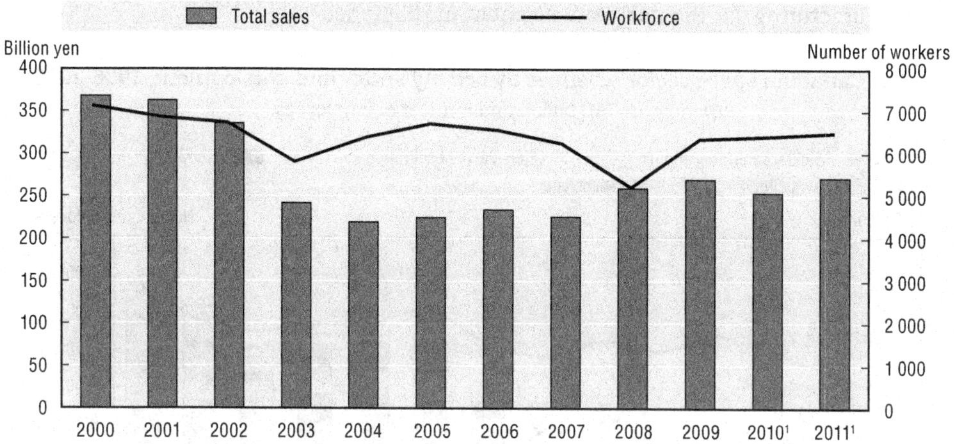

Source: Adapted from SJAC, 2010 in OECD (2011), *The Space Economy at a Glance 2011*, OECD Publishing, *http://dx.doi.org/10.1787/9789264111790-en*, p. 61.

StatLink http://dx.doi.org/10.1787/888932576643

Figure 6.3. **Revenues of Chinese companies involved in spacecraft manufacturing and number of employees, 1995-2009**

Billions of yuan and number of employees

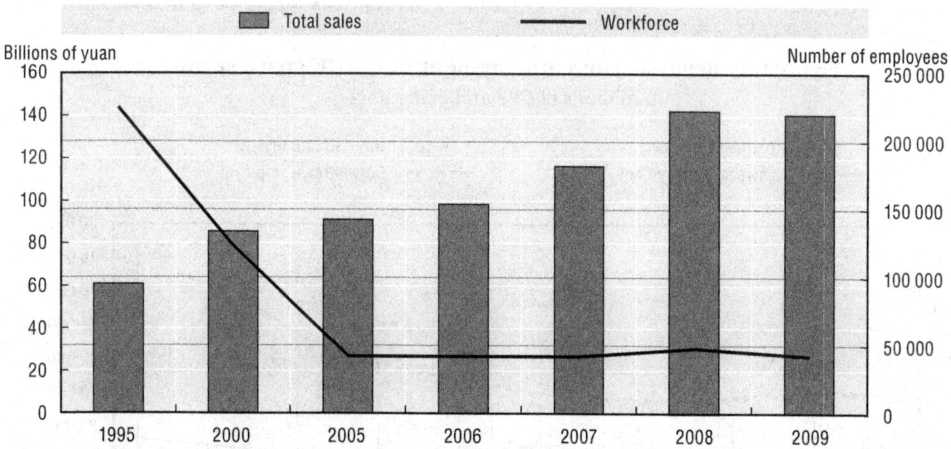

Source: Based on data from the Chinese National Bureau of Statistics data, 2010 in OECD (2011), *The Space Economy at a Glance 2011*, OECD Publishing, *http://dx.doi.org/10.1787/9789264111790-en*, p. 103.

StatLink http://dx.doi.org/10.1787/888932576662

Other surveys include larger segments of the value chain to map services derived from the uses of space assets. This is the case for countries with small space manufacturing sectors, but active on specific segments (*e.g.* robotics) and homes to dynamic space applications providers, like Canada and the United Kingdom. The two figures below provide data on their respective space sector, which in that case encompasses more than just actors in space manufacturing (*i.e.* the upstream segment in UK statistics).

Figure 6.4. **Canadian space sector revenues by activity sector and employment, 1996-2008**

Revenues in CAD billion and number of employees

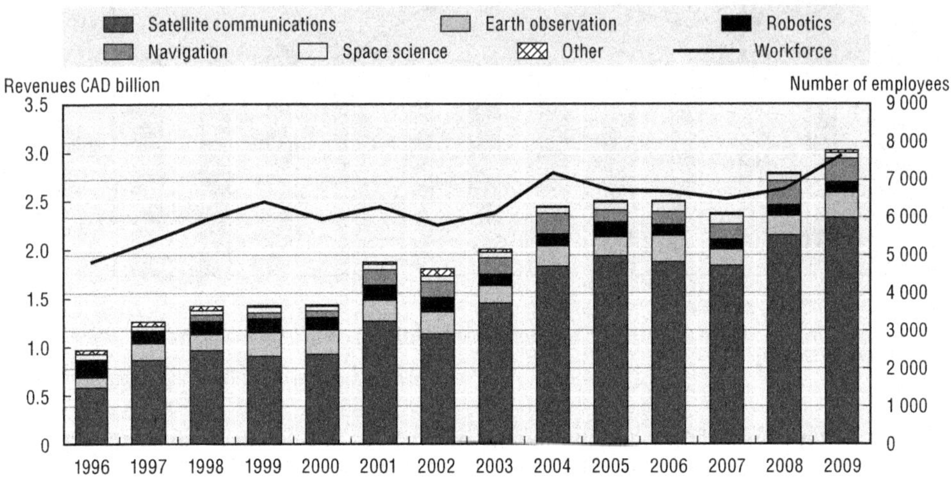

Source: CSA, 2010 in OECD (2011), *The Space Economy at a Glance 2011*, OECD Publishing, *http://dx.doi.org/10.1787/9789264111790-en*, p. 95.

StatLink http://dx.doi.org/10.1787/888932576681

Figure 6.5. **Revenues and employment in the UK space sector**

In millions of GBP and percentage

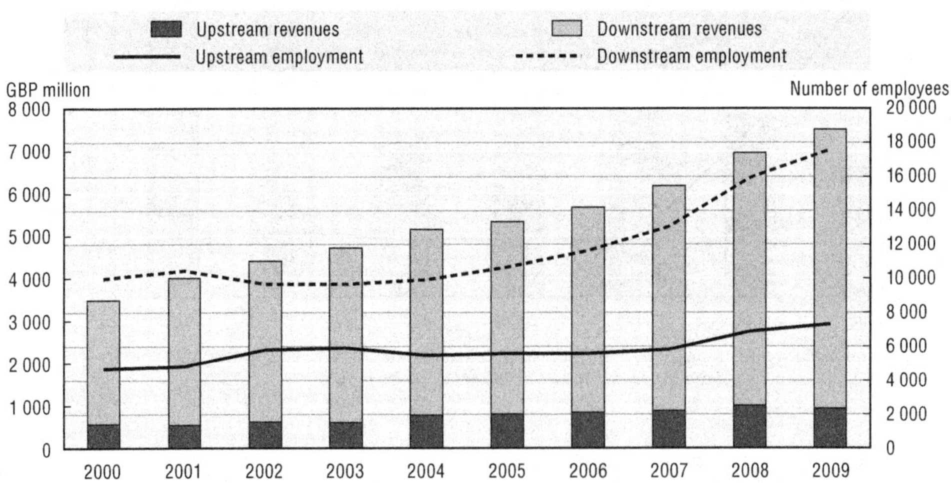

Source: UK National Space Agency, 2010 in OECD (2011), *The Space Economy at a Glance 2011*, OECD Publishing, *http://dx.doi.org/10.1787/9789264111790-en*, p. 97.

StatLink http://dx.doi.org/10.1787/888932576700

When collecting and examining space manufacturing data, in addition to common methodological questions seen in Chapter 4 (*i.e.* evaluating data sources, taking into account exchange rates and double counting) the following issues arise:

- Data providers use very diverse methodologies and statistical categories to collect data, which make international comparability challenging. But they also have different timelines (based often on different fiscal years) and sometimes do not conduct surveys regularly. For example, Eurospace, The Canadian Space Agency, and the Society of Japanese Aerospace Companies all conduct annual surveys of the space sector. On the contrary, the UK National Space Agency, working with diverse private data providers, conducts industry surveys every two to three years.
- When surveys examine in more details the space sector's value chain, they can provide annual data on prime contractors and major subcontractors (*e.g.* Eurospace surveys). But frequently, estimates for the space manufacturing industry often lack:
  - Revenues from lower-tier subcontractors and vendors.
  - Revenues for specific associated activities of non-engineering firms (marketing, finance, public relations, etc.).

Since the first issue of *The Space Economy at a Glance* (2007), more data providers have made a move to make their data more transparent (*e.g.* mentioning current versus constant currencies, using inflation deflators). Efforts are also ongoing inside the International Astronautical Federation to discuss statistical methodological issues to promote and facilitate international data comparisons in the space community.

Space-based applications and derived services

There is a wide diversity of space-related products and services, many of which are commercial in nature, while others have known market failure and require support from governments to sustain their public good impacts. Space-based applications all require specific satellite capacities to function, such as a satellite data link or signal (*i.e.* telecommunications, navigation, Earth observation).

Telecommunications represent the main commercial space market, benefiting from growing mass markets (satellite television broadcasting) and a robust demand from institutional users (defence, new customers in the developing world, development of anchor contracts). The geopositioning market is also a growing new segment building on satellite positioning, navigation and timing signals (with products such as the now common car-navigation). It represents some USD 15 billion in revenue in 2009. With the advances in smartphones and other mobile products, all offering geopositioning capabilities, more growth is expected. Another field of applications include the satellite Earth observation sector, a market valued in 2009 at some USD 900 million to USD 1.2 billion. Finally others, derived from the main space manufacturing and space applications sectors, include for example the space insurance industry, which generates around USD 750-800 million a year. As a case study, the satellite telecommunications sector is reviewed in more details in the next paragraphs.

Satellite communications' services have historically been aggregated in official statistics with other data. Since the latest ISIC revision, a new international classification for satellite communications have been created, but it takes time and efforts to include new categories in national surveys. At international levels, both the International Telecommunication Union (ITU) and the OECD publish annually indicators on communications and satellite communications indicators, for which data times series already exist, as shown in the table below (OECD, 2007). In general, private surveys and consulting reports provide the most up-to-date information on the communications market, although difference in proprietary definitions and methodologies can cause difficulties to data users (*e.g.* revenues in current or constant prices. See Chapter 4 for review of methodological caveats).

Table 6.1. **ITU indicators including data about satellite usage**

ITU Code	Indicators	Description
965m	Total number of multi-channel TV subscribers	This is the total number of multi-channel TV subscribers (both terrestrial and satellite); (see below: 965m = 965c + 965s).
965c	Number of terrestrial multi-channel TV subscribers	Number of terrestrial multi-channel TV such as cable TV, digital terrestrial TV, Microwave Multi-point Distribution systems (MMDS) and Satellite Master Antenna Television (SMATV) subscribers.
965s	Direct to Home satellite antenna subscribers	The number of subscribers to a home satellite antenna that can receive television broadcasting directly from satellites.
965cp	Homes passed by multi-channel TV	Number of households that have a multi-channel (both terrestrial and satellite) television connection whether they are subscribing or not.
4213ob	Other fixed broadband Internet subscribers	Internet subscribers using fixed broadband technologies (other than DSL, cable modem and leased lines) to access the Internet. This includes technologies such as satellite broadband Internet, Fibre-to-the-home Internet access, Ethernet LANs, fixed-wireless access, Wireless Local Area Network, WiMAX, etc. Speeds should be equal to, or greater than, 256 kbit/s, in one or both directions. It would exclude those users of temporary broadband access (*e.g.*, roaming between PWLAN hotspots), and those with Internet access via mobile cellular networks.

Source: Adapted from ITU (2010), "World Telecommunication/ICT Development Report 2010", *Monitoring The WSIS Targets: A mid-term review*, International Telecommunications Union, Geneva.

An example of aggregated data is presented in the next figure. Since satellite broadband is for the time being relatively marginal compared to other broadband technologies, it is often included in the most recent broadband technologies category, which includes fibre broadband connections, broadband wireless access, and satellite broadband. These "other broadband" technologies (compared with more known technologies such as cable, DSL, etc.) which are regrouped under the ITU Code 4213ob (see Table 6.1) make up only 6% of all broadband lines in the OECD area, although the percentage is growing steadily, as shown in the figure below.

Figure 6.6. **Growth in communication access paths by technology, 2003-05**

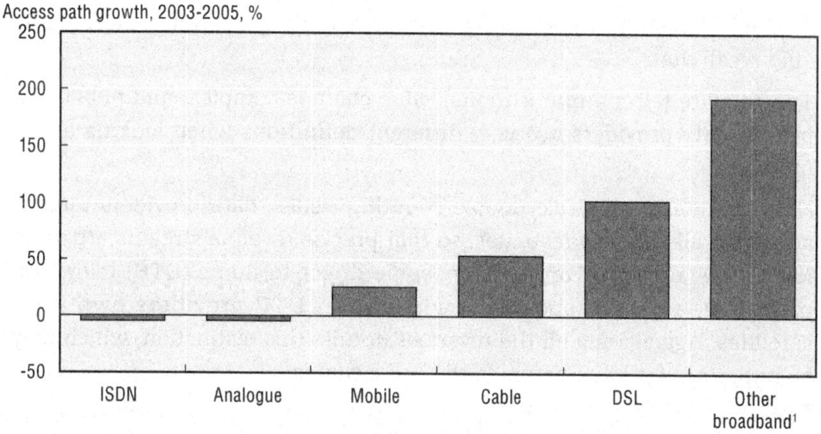

1. Other broadband include fibre broadband connections, broadband wireless access, and satellite broadband.

Source: OECD (2007), *OECD Communications Outlook 2007*, OECD Publishing, *http://dx.doi.org/10.1787/comms_outlook-2007-en.*

StatLink http://dx.doi.org/10.1787/888932576719

As another example, the table below presents market data for a particular segment of the satellite telecommunications value chain: the "very small aperture terminal" or VSAT industry. A VSAT is a two-way satellite ground station with a dish antenna, used for communications (fixed or on the move in the case of mobile maritime communications), to transmit narrowband data (such as credit card transactions), and now extensively to receive and send broadband data. It is estimated there are more than 500 000 terminals installed in more than 120 countries and the number is growing, as the provision of satellite Internet access to remote locations and mobile users expands (Global VSAT Forum, 2011).

Table 6.2. **Data on the VSAT industry (2010)**

Enterprise and Broadband Star Data Systems	
Total Number of Enterprise VSAT Terminals Ordered	2 276 348
Total Number of VSATs Shipped	2 220 280
Total Number of Sites in Service	1 271 900
Market Shipments 3 Year CAGR	13.1%
VSAT Revenues	
All Service Revenues	USD 5.46 billion
TDMA & DAMA Hardware Revenues	USD 964.0 million

Source: Comsys (2010), *Annual VSAT Report, 11th edition*, Report prepared by Simon Bull, Comsys, London.

When collecting/interpreting data for satellite communications, one should recall that:

- The satellite telecommunications' value chain is complex, and public and private data providers use very different definitions when looking at the industry.
- Notwithstanding possible double counting issues, data providers tend to aggregate all industry revenues, so that precise revenue streams are often lost in the analysis. For example, some direct-to-home (DTH) television providers lease transponders, while other DTH providers own their satellites. Aggregating all the revenues occults this distinction, which may be important for other actors in the value chains.

International trade in selected space products

Not many space products and services are fully commercial, as most are strategic in nature and not freely traded (*see section 2.2 concerning space products in international statistical classifications*). In *The Space Economy at a Glance 2011*, a partial overview of existing trade data is provided by examining the exports of one commodity code with significant space components from the International Trade in Commodity Statistics (ITCS) database (OECD, 2011). The Commodity Code used is 7925 "Spacecraft (including satellites) and spacecraft launch vehicles". Based on available ITCS trade data, France, the United States, Belgium, Italy and Germany lead the exports of spacecraft and spacecraft launch vehicles. Concerning importers, a vast diversity of OECD and non-OECD countries appear, reflecting the emergence of new actors in space activities. But the data remain limited.

In most countries, the information on imports and exports of goods come from customs declarations (United Nations Statistical Commission, 2008). Due to confidentiality issues, countries may not report some of their detailed trade, and imports reported by one country may not coincide with exports reported by its trading partners. Differences can be due to various factors including national trade valuation (imports/exports including or excluding "cost, insurance, and freight"), differences in inclusions/ exclusions of particular commodities, or timing.

These official trade data need therefore to be completed by other data, gathered by space agencies and industry associations, particularly for countries that are strong exporters of space technologies and/or services. For example Canada's trading partners are tracked by the Canadian Space Agency annually, as shown in the figure below.

Figure 6.7. **Canadian space sector's export revenue by destination, 1996-2009**

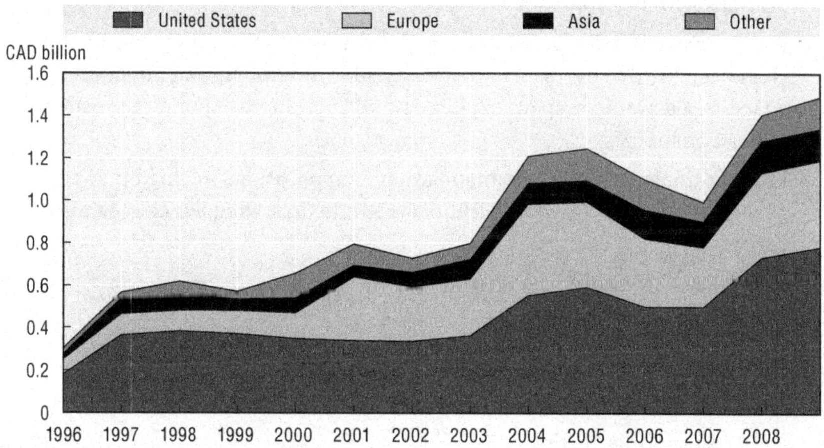

Source: Canadian Space Agency, 2010 in OECD (2011), *The Space Economy at a Glance 2011*, OECD Publishing, *http://dx.doi.org/10.1787/9789264111790-en*, p. 95.

StatLink http://dx.doi.org/10.1787/888932576738

Innovation for future economic growth: patents

A patent is a legal title granting its holder the exclusive right to make use of an invention for a limited area and time, it is part of his/her intellectual property rights (IPR). An invention needs to fulfill three criteria to be granted a patent: 1) novelty, 2) inventive step, and 3) industrial applicability. All patent applications and granted patents are published. They provide a useful indicator of innovative developments in all areas of technology, and they can indicate the level of innovative activity in a particular market, region or country. In the field of space technology under-representation of innovative activity within patent systems may be more marked since much dual-use space research and development is subject to secrecy.

In *The Space Economy at a Glance 2011*, space-related patents were identified using a combination of codes from the International Patent

Classification (IPC) and key word searches in the patent title (OECD, 2011). The classification B64G: "Cosmonautics; vehicles or equipment thereof" was used as a starting point. It covers a large array of space-related systems and applications (including satellites; launchers; components; radio or other wave systems for navigation or tracking; simulators). The box below summarises the methodology used to extract data from the OECD Patents Database.

Box 6.1. **Defining space-related patents**

Space-related patents are defined using a mixture of International Patent Classification (IPC) codes and keywords. More work is ongoing to refine the definitions with keywords.

- B64G "Cosmonautics; vehicles or Equipment thereof" is the principle IPC class used, which covers technology related to developing and maintaining space-based systems; space exploration and peripheral equipment related to cosmonautics.
- In order to also capture patents relating to applications relying on space-based technology, patent applications with the following IPC classes were chosen:
  - B64 Aircraft; Aviation; Cosmonautics.
  - C06 Explosives; Matches.
  - F41 Weapons.
  - F42 Ammunition; Blasting.
  - G01 Measuring; Testing.
  - G08 Signalling.
  - H01 Basic electric elements.
  - H02 Generation, conversion, or distribution of electric power.
  - H03 Basic Electronic Circuitry.
  - H04 Electric Communication Technique.
  - H05 Electric techniques not otherwise provided for.

Using the different IPC classes mentioned above, the following keywords were used:

For general satellite technologies patents:

- "satellite"
- "spacecraft"
- "rocket"
- "space"
- "launcher"

Box 6.1. **Defining space-related patents** *(cont.)*

For satellite navigation patents:

- "GPS"
- "navigation"
- "positioning"
- "timing"

For satellite Earth observation patents:

- "earth observation"
- "remote sensing"
- "meteorology "
- "optical "
- "radar "
- "lidar "

For satellite communications patents:

- "communication + satellite"
- "multiplex"
- "broadcast + satellite"
- "broadband + satellite"
- "television + satellite"
- "transponder"

In this analysis no adjustments have been made for inventions filed at both European Patent Office (EPO) and United States Patent and Trademark Office (USPTO), although the results also include space-related patent applications filed under the Patent Co-operation Treaty (PCT).

The PCT offers applicants the possibility to seek patent rights in a large number of countries by filing a single international application with a single patent office (receiving office). Data on the number of PCT patent applications are more internationally comparable because they avoid home country advantages and cover inventions that are potentially worth patenting in more than one country. A methodological issue concerns the visible downturn of patent applications after 2001 (see Figure below). This is mainly due to delays in updating patent databases and also the time-lag at the USPTO between the application of a patent and its granting. Thus, the downturn should not be misconstrued as a recession in terms of space-related patenting activities. As in the case of other sectors, space patents tend to become international in nature. The Canadian Space Agency, in its annual space industry survey, is also seeing more multi-country patents being reported over the years.

Figure 6.8. **Evolution of space-related patents, 1980-2007**

Number of patents filed by patent offices and priority date

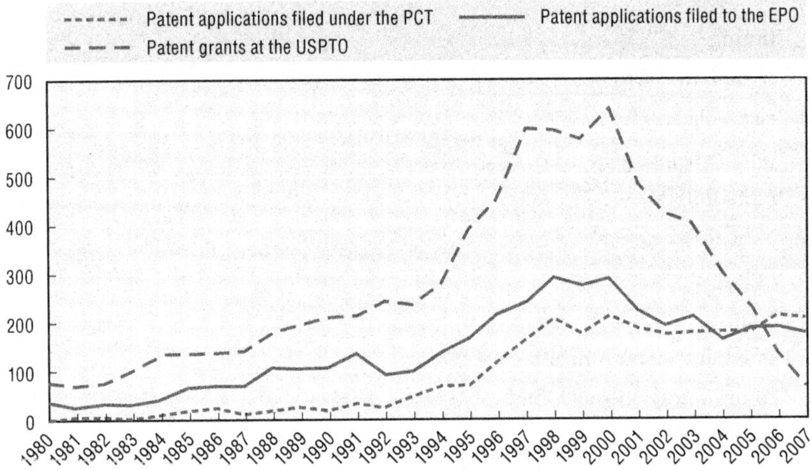

Source: OECD, *Patent Database*, August 2010 in OECD (2011), *The Space Economy at a Glance 2011*, OECD Publishing, *http://dx.doi.org/10.1787/9789264111790-en*, p. 71.

StatLink http://dx.doi.org/10.1787/888932576757

The number of space-related patents has almost quadrupled in fifteen years when looking at the applications filed under the PCT. Analysis of patents provides some insight into innovative activities concerning the electrical and mechanical machinery and equipment required for space-based systems (satellites, launchers) as well as the downstream applications, such as telecommunications navigation systems. It remains that patent data have advantages and disadvantages for illustrating inventive activities, as reflected in the table below.

Another possibility to track innovation is to use bibliometric (or publication) data. Bibliometric data are used to capture research and development activities closer to basic science while patent data highlight activities further downstream from basic science. The multitude of articles, notes, letters and reviews that are published daily in scientific journals, along the numerous citations between these publications, provide a paper trail of the development, structural relationships, and diffusion of scientific knowledge. Publications and their citations are also often used as indicators for the performance of the public research system of countries or specific universities and institutes. Publication databases are very large and can

Table 6.3. Patent data's advantages and disadvantages in reflecting inventive activities

Advantages

- Patents cover a broad range of technologies for which there are sometimes few other sources of data (*i.e.* nanotechnology).
- Patents have a close (if imperfect) link to invention. Most significant inventions from businesses are patented, whether based on R&D or not.
- Each patent document contains detailed information on the invention process: a reasonably complete description of the invention, the technology field concerned, the inventors (name, address), the applicant (owner), citations to previous patents and scientific articles to which the invention relates, etc. The amount of patent data available to researchers is huge. More than one million patents are applied for worldwide each year, providing unique information on the progress of invention. Patent data are public, unlike survey data which are usually protected by statistical secrecy laws.
- The spatial and temporal coverage of patent data is unique. Patent data are available from all countries with a patent system. They are available – sometimes in electronic form – from first patent systems, which go back to the 19th century in most OECD countries.
- Patent data are quite readily available from national and regional patent offices. The marginal cost for the statistician is much lower than for conducting surveys although it is sometimes still significant (data need to be cleaned, formatted, etc.). Unlike survey data, collection of patent statistics does not put any supplementary burden on the reporting unit (*e.g.* business) because the data are already collected by patent offices in order to process applications.

Disadvantages

- Not all inventions are patented. Inventions with few economic possibilities may not justify the cost of patenting. Strategic considerations may lead the inventor to prefer alternative protection (secrecy), with the result that the patent data do not reflect such inventions (*e.g.* Pavitt, 1988).
- The propensity to file patent applications differs significantly across technical fields. For instance, in the electronics industry (*e.g.* semiconductors) a patented invention can be surrounded by patent applications on incremental variations of the invention, with a view to deterring the entry of new competitors and to negotiating advantageous cross-licensing deals with competitors. As a result of this "patent flooding" strategy, some technical fields have a larger number of patents than others. Companies' propensity to patent also differs: new or small and medium-sized enterprises (SMEs) – notably those that lack large-scale production – have more difficulty covering the costs of a patent (although national policies attempt to deal with this problem by providing SMEs with subsidies or discount rates).
- Several studies have shown that the value distribution of patents may be skewed. Many patents have no industrial application (hence, are of little or no value to society), whereas a few have very high value. Nonetheless, the disclosure of information represents a benefit for society, as it increases the stock of knowledge. With such heterogeneity, simple patent counts can be misleading. This is not specific to patents, but a reflection of a prominent feature of the inventive process which also applies to R&D expenditure (which often results in little success, but sometimes in huge success).
- Differences in patent law and practices around the world limit the comparability of patent statistics across countries. It is therefore preferable to use homogenous patent data (coming from a single patent office or single set of patent offices).
- Changes in patent laws over the years call for caution when analyzing trends over time. The protection afforded patentees worldwide has been stepped up since the early 1980s, and companies are therefore more inclined to patent than before. The list of technologies covered has grown longer over time and in some countries now includes software and genetic sequences, which were previously excluded. Other variables, such as office administration, can have a substantial impact on patent counts, notably patents granted, during a particular time period.
- Patent data are complex, as they are generated by complex legal and economic processes. It is therefore important to take into account all of these factors when compiling and interpreting patent data, as failing to do so could lead to erroneous conclusions.

Source: OECD (2009), *OECD Patent Statistics Manual*, OECD Publishing, *http://dx.doi.org/10.1787/9789264056442-en.*

sometimes be poorly indexed as they collect data from various journals with different indexing systems and nomenclatures. The delimitation of subsets of publications of specific scientific fields are typically been done using advanced keyword search algorithms that also consider cross-citation patterns and expert opinion. This type of activity would be useful to try and track innovation derived from space research.

Box 6.2. **Advantages and limitations of bibliometric data**

Advantages:

- Publications are closely linked to research activity.
- They have been subject to peer-review for quality control.
- They cover a broad range of scientific disciplines.
- Publication data are available as long time series.
- They are publicly available at a low cost.

Limitations:

- Publication databases are biased in favour of English-language journals as the mainstream outlets.
- They combine different journal-specific databases whereby targeted searches are cumbersome.
- Publication data only cover the codified aspects of scientific research.
- Citation data may not only reflect genuine interrelationships and quality of research.
- Publication behaviour and propensities may vary significantly across disciplinary fields.

Source: Palmberg *et al.* (2009), "Nanotechnology: An Overview Based on Indicators and Statistics", *OECD Science, Technology and Industry Working Papers*, No. 2009/07.

This chapter has highlighted a number of indicators with their associated measurement issues, but there are many more as demonstrated by the ones presented in the publication *The Space Economy at A Glance 2011*. Future revisions to this *Handbook* will most likely feature more indicators.

References

Comsys (2010), *Annual VSAT Report, 11th edition*, Report prepared by Simon Bull, Comsys, London.

Global VSAT Forum (2011), *About the VSAT Industry, website*, London. Available: *www.gvf.org* [*Accessed March*].

ITU (2010), *World Telecommunication/ICT Development Report* 2010, Monitoring The WSIS Targets: A mid-term review, International Telecommunications Union, Geneva.

OECD (2007), *OECD Communications Outlook 2007*, OECD Publishing, *http://dx.doi.org/10.1787/comms_outlook-2007-en*.

OECD (2009), *OECD Patent Statistics Manual*, OECD Publishing, *http://dx.doi.org/10.1787/9789264056442-en*.

OECD (2011), *The Space Economy at A Glance* 2011, OECD Publishing, *http://dx.doi.org/10.1787/9789264111790-en*.

Palmberg, C., H. Dernis and C. Miguet (2009), "Nanotechnology: An Overview Based on Indicators and Statistics", *OECD Science, Technology and Industry Working Papers*, No. 2009/07.

United Nations Statistical Commission (2008), *Updated System of National Accounts (SNA): Chapter 14: The supply and use tables and goods and services account*, United Nations Economic and Social Council, Statistical Commission, Thirty-ninth session, 26-29 February 2008, Item 3(d) of the provisional agenda, New York.

PART II

Chapter 7

Measuring Socio-economic Impacts from Space Activities

This chapter reviews various types of socio-economic impacts derived from the development of space activities. The main message is that many space-based services have positive impacts on society, but issues concerning economic data definitions and methodologies have to be resolved to allow the benefits to be identified and quantified more precisely.

Defining socio-economic impacts from space programmes

The investments in space programmes are often justified by the scientific, technological, industrial and security capabilities they bring. The wish to develop a specialisation may allow a country to participate later on in large space programmes because of its expertise (*e.g.* Canada's expertise in robotics and radar imagery; Norway's expertise in developing satellite telecommunications in difficult environments, such as platforms at sea).

Space investments can also provide socio-economic returns such as increased industrial activity, and bring cost efficiencies and productivity gains in other fields (*e.g.* weather forecasting, telemedicine, environmental monitoring and agriculture previsions). Several space applications have reached technical maturity and have become the sources of new commercial downstream activities, sometimes far removed from the initial space research and development. For example, the growth of positioning, navigation and timing applications, which rely on satellite signals, has spurred new commercial markets (*e.g.* GPS chipsets in smartphones). But as Einstein wrote: "Not everything that counts, can be counted." This is also true for the diversity of socio-economic impacts derived from space activities.

The analytical work done so far on impacts has tended to be based on small-scale/national studies rather than comprehensive exercises repeated over time and based on official statistics. Despite these limitations, research conducted by OECD /IFP has shown that impacts analysed so far can be categorised in four different segments: creation of new commercial products and services (including "indirect industrial effects" from space industry contracts, meaning new exports or new activities outside the space sector), productivity/efficiency gains in diverse economic sectors (*e.g.* fisheries, airlines), economic growth regionally and nationally, and cost avoidances (*e.g.* floods). One major challenge concerns specific measurement issues associated with the "social" dimensions of the impacts, like for example the reduction of the digital divide in rural areas thanks to satellite telecommunications. These are important and valuable social impacts, for which measurement requires further work. The following sections briefly review some of the impacts that have been detected so far.

Figure 7.1. **Review of possible impacts derived from investments in space programme**

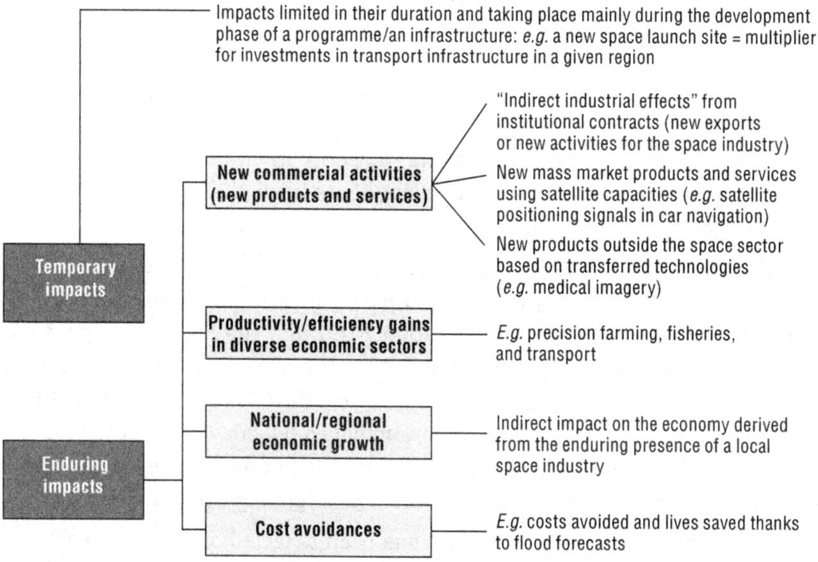

Source: OECD (2011), *The Space Economy at a Glance 2011*, OECD Publishing, *http://dx.doi.org/10.1787/9789264111790-en*, p. 79.

Box 7.1. **Space applications and cost benefit analysis**

The most common economic measurement for any technology's value is the calculation of benefits to costs. In theory, to calculate the ratio, it is necessary to divide the benefits (*e.g.* improved productivity, decreased cost of operations, increased revenue and better customer satisfaction rates when applicable) by the costs of deploying the system (*e.g.* hardware, software, maintenance, training and so forth). However space systems are by nature multifaceted and rely often on lengthy research and development. The challenge of putting a monetary value on the technologies and services they deliver remains a complex and often subjective exercise. As discussed in OECD (2008), monetary or financial valuation methods fall into three basic types, each with its own repertoire of associated measurement issues and none of them entirely satisfactory on its own. They include: direct market valuation (*e.g.* market pricing), indirect market valuation (*e.g.* replacement cost) and survey-based valuation techniques (*i.e.* contingent valuation and group valuation). One option is to use several of these methods in parallel to test assumptions and the resulting impacts of a given space application. Ongoing work in OECD is devoted to conducting case studies on selected space applications, in order to provide a source of comparative national experiences and lessons learned when trying to apply the different methodologies to the study of impacts.

New commercial/industrial activities

In a majority of countries, space programmes are contracted out to industry. The ability of firms to secure new customers or create new activities has been studied over the years, and although impacts may vary depending on the country and the level of its specialisation (*e.g.* applications versus manufacturing), there are several examples of positive industrial and economic returns from space investments, not only in countries with large space manufacturing industry but also in countries with smaller specialised space programmes. Follow some examples quoted in OECD (2011):

- Norway – which has a small but active space programme – has detected a positive multiplier effect since the 1990s, *i.e.* in 2009, for each million Norwegian kroner of governmental support through the European Space Agency (ESA) or national support programmes, the Norwegian space sector companies have on average generated an additional turnover of NOK 4.7 million, usually as new exports or new activities outside the space sector. This spin-off effect factor is expected to climb further as Norwegian space sector develops new products and services (Norwegian Space Centre, 2010).
- In Belgium, the same type of multiplier has been detected. In 2010, for each EUR million of governmental support through ESA, it was found that EUR 1.4 million have been generated by the Belgian space industry (Capron *et al.*, 2010).
- In Denmark, where some 25 companies are active in the space sector, each EUR million of Danish contributions to the European Space Agency has generated a turnover of EUR 3.7 million on average. Increased competencies within space activities through involvement in ESA projects is seen by the industry as facilitating the development of competencies in other sectors than the space sector (Danish Agency for Science Technology and Innovation, 2008).

R&D and innovation play an important role in many industries, although the derived competitiveness seems to be strongly affected by the size of the domestic market, this is true also for the space sector. However spillovers are sometimes as important as the direct effects. And this is an argument for public support of R&D in private firms (Fagerberg, 1996). The studies conducted by these countries have used different methodologies (*e.g.* input-outputs analysis, surveys). Already in the 1990s, the BETA (Bureau d'Économie Théorique et Appliquée) of the University Louis Pasteur had developed a methodology extensively applied to assess indirect economic effects of European Space Agency contracts in European member countries (BETA, 1989, 1997). Results showed already positive effects of ESA contracts for firms active in Europe and in Canada (Cohendet *et al.*, 2002).

Concerning space technology transfers to diverse economic sectors, many studies of "spin-offs" have been conducted in the United States since the 1960s (such as outputs from NASA's Apollo programme), focusing on the transfers from space-related hardware and know-how to other sectors (NASA, 2010). The value of spin-offs is however not easily quantifiable, and at times oversold concepts have been detrimental (*e.g.* Teflon as space technology). There are currently more than 1 600 NASA-derived technologies that have been transferred to other sectors, bringing efficiency gains particularly in medical imagery (*e.g.* Hubble telescope's optics used for increased precision in microinvasive arthroscopic surgery).

Box 7.2. **Science and space exploration as key drivers of space programmes**

Countries with space programmes are increasingly investing in down-to-earth space applications (*e.g.* telecommunications, earth observation) for strategic and economic reasons. Nevertheless, science and space exploration remain key drivers for investments and constitute an intensive activity for major space agencies and industry (OECD, 2011). Space sciences and planetary missions have developed markedly over the years, with new actors joining in. This trend is reflected in the current and planned robotic exploration missions of the solar system, in which the United States, Canada, Europe, Japan, China and India are active players. In addition to those robotic missions targeted at extraterrestrial bodies, more than a dozen space science satellites are orbiting the earth, while dozens of ground-based telescopes are managed internationally. More countries than ever are also investing in indigenous human spaceflight capabilities. Over the past couple of years, a new generation of professional astronauts was selected in the United States, the European Space Agency member states, Canada and China.

Regional/national economic growth

The macroeconomic impacts of space programmes at regional or even national levels have been measured in countries with significant space industry (manufacturing and/or services), such as the United States, France and most recently in the United Kingdom. Economic impacts analysis is not unique to the space sector, and similar studies on economic spillovers are regularly conducted for the automobile industry, the oil industry or the defence sector (*e.g.* economic effects of large military bases).

- In France, several regional studies were conducted over the years on French Guyana, an overseas department where the European spaceport is located (INSEE, 2010). The share of value added due to space activities accounted for 21% of French Guyana's GDP on average during the decade 1965-75. With the advent of commercial launcher and Arianespace, the economic importance of space has risen sharply in the early 1990s (28.7% in 1991). It began to decline in 1994 (25.7%), and accelerated again in 2002-03 with new Ariane 5 launches (INSEE, 2008). French Guyana exports predominantly consist of space transportation services sales by Arianespace. The ratio of exports to GDP is much higher than what is found in other exports of French Guyana.

- In the United States, home of the biggest space industry in terms of employment and revenues, the most recent FAA study on the wider national economic impacts of the US commercial space activities has shown a rather stable multiplier ratio since 2002 (FAA, 2010). In 2009, for every dollar spent commercial space transportation industry, USD 4.9 resulted in indirect and induced economic impact. Using the same modeling techniques as the ones used for the aeronautic industry, the results show that many economic sectors may be impacted by commercial space activities, as they provide goods and services, directly or indirectly, to the space industry. In 2009, the Information Services industry was the most affected group in terms of additional economic activity, earnings and jobs, generating over USD 65.4 billion of revenue, over USD 15.3 billion in earnings, and creating 213 230 jobs.
- In the United Kingdom, where the downstream space services' sector have been growing steadily (boosted by the satellite communications sector), a national economic impacts study was also conducted recently. Including both upstream and downstream actors (from satellite manufacturers to operators and providers of services), the space industry's value-added multiplier on the British economy has been estimated to be 1.91 and the employment multiplier to be 3.34 (Figure 14.2). The space industry's direct value-added contribution to GDP was estimated at some GBP 3.8 billion and the indirect economic impacts amounted to an additional GBP 3.3 billion (*i.e.* space industry's spending on non-space UK inputs). The total UK-based employment supported by the space industry was estimated to be 83 000 in 2009 (UK Space Agency, 2010).

The American and French economic impact studies apply different input/ output methods, while the United Kingdom analysis is based on the results of industry survey responses. The FAA uses the Regional Input-Output Modelling System (RIMS II) developed by the Department of Commerce, Bureau of Economic Analysis. The French national statistical office INSEE has used different impacts methodologies over time. Input-output analysis specifically shows how industries are linked together through supplying inputs for the output of an economy. Factors that can be used to construct indicators of productivity are for example employment, expenditures, income, production of goods and services and competitiveness. Such factors are of interest at both the national and regional levels. Results of these analyses are derived from macroeconomic data such as changes in GDP, which can then be compared to changes in capital. The challenge when interpreting the material is to find the causal linkages between the programme/ infrastructure investments and the rise in productivity. However, the findings of these studies are sometimes contentious, and highly dependent on the choice and evaluation of appropriate variables over long periods, as well as the calculations used to assess their cause and effect mechanisms.

Efficiency/productivity gains

The amount of efficiency and productivity gains derived from the use of space applications across very diverse sectors of the economy keeps growing over the years. From agriculture to energy, institutional actors and private companies are using satellite signals and imagery with usually positive returns. Satellites can also play a key role in providing communications infrastructure rapidly to areas lacking any ground infrastructure, contributing to link rural and isolated areas with urbanised centres:

- Positioning and navigation efficiencies. Adoption of satellite navigation-related technologies in fishing fleets began in the mid-1980s, and general technology rollout and adoption began in the mid-1990s all over the world. Based on efficiency gains studies, the fishing power of the commercial Australian fleet increased since the uptake of GPS and plotters. The cumulative addition to fishing output that were conservatively attributed to the use of GPS plotters was estimated at 4.14% of output in 2007, equivalent to around AUD 88 million at 2007 prices (OECD, 2008b).
- Higher perspectives from space. The specific topographic perspectives brought by earth observation and navigation satellites allow cost-efficiencies. In India, a large petrochemical group uses remote sensing to plan several pipeline routings for the transportation and distribution of natural gas/hydrocarbons. Building a geographic information system with imagery from the Indian Cartosat-1 satellite and cadastral data, the company's field work time was reduced from 90% to less than 15% from previous conventional surveys (usually only 1.5 to 2 km were covered per day compared with more than a hundred of kilometres with satellites). Updates in the imagery database will help monitor the pipeline routing areas and create long-term time series (Indian Space Research Organisation, 2010).

In the case of space applications, the study of productivity gains are often conducted as ad hoc reports, therefore methodologies may vary and render difficult international comparability. The OECD is building up a database of existing indicators, as to provide access to data and methodological information.

Judging from the different types of impacts presented, space applications and diverse programmes in the space sector have been the focus of many socio-economic studies over the years. However, all such studies face inherent limitations, very similar to those in other types of public R&D impacts analysis (see box below). When assessing the results of these studies there is often a reluctance to link socio-economic outcome measures too directly to a research programmes or a given space application, as there are many intervening steps that may distort the causal link. One option is to use several assessment methods in parallel to test assumptions and the resulting impacts of a given space application or programme.

Box 7.3. Challenges encountered when analysing the impacts of R&D programmes

- **Causality.** There is typically no direct link between a research investment and an impact. Research inputs generate particular outputs that will then have an impact on society. As it is indirect, this relationship is difficult to identify and measure. It is also almost impossible to isolate the influence of one specific factor (research output) on one impact, because the latter is in general affected by several factors that are difficult to control for.
- **Sector specificities.** Creation and channelling of output to the end-user will differ depending on the research field and industry. This renders ineffective the use of one single framework for assessment.
- **Multiple benefits.** A basic research impact may have several dimensions, not all of which are easily identified.
- **Identification of users.** Identification of all end-users who benefit from the research outputs can be difficult and/or costly, especially in the case of basic research.
- **Complex transfer mechanisms.** It is difficult to identify and describe all the potential mechanisms for transferring research results to society. Some studies have identified mechanisms of transfer between businesses or between universities and businesses. These models are mainly empirical and often reveal little of the full impact on society of such transfers.
- **Lack of appropriate indicators.** Since appropriate benefit categories, relevant transfer mechanisms and end-users are often lacking, it is also difficult to define and measure appropriate impact indicators related to specific research outputs.
- **International spillovers.** The existence of knowledge spillovers has been well documented and demonstrated. As a result, specific impacts could be partially the result of internationally performed research instead of national research investments.
- **Time lags.** Different research investments vary in the time it takes them to have an impact on society. Any measurement may thus prove premature, especially in the case of basic research.
- **Interdisciplinary output.** Research outputs, *e.g.* improved skills, may have different impacts, and it may be difficult to identify them all in order to evaluate the contribution of the specific output, let alone that of the research investment.
- **Valuation.** In many cases it is difficult to come up with a monetary value of the impacts so as to make them comparable. Even if identifiable, noneconomic impacts may be difficult to value. There have been some attempts to translate some of these impacts (such as the economic savings associated with a healthy population or the calculation of opinion values) into economic terms, but these have typically remained partial and open to subjectivity.

Source: OECD (2008), "Assessing the Socio-economic Impacts of Public R&D: Recent Practices and Perspectives", in OECD, *OECD Science, Technology and Industry Outlook 2008*, OECD Publishing, *http://dx.doi.org/10.1787/sti_outlook-2008-41-en.*

References

BETA (1989), *Indirect Economic Effects of ESA Contracts on the Canadian Economy*, Final Report, France.

BETA (1997), *Les effets économiques indirects des contrats de l'ASE sur l'économie canadienne* (deuxième étude, 1988-1997), rapport final, Canada.

Capron, H., D. Baudewyns and M. Depelchinn (2010), *Les établissements scientifiques fédéraux, Collection Économie*, Université Libre de Bruxelles (in French). Brussels.

Cohendet, P. *et al.* (2002), "Technological Transfers from the European Space Programs: A Dynamic View and Comparison with Other R&D Projects", *Journal of Technology Transfer*, 27.

Danish Agency for Science Technology and Innovation (2008), *Evaluation of Danish Industrial Activities in the European Space Agency (ESA): Assessment of the economic impacts of the Danish ESA-membership*, Copenhague, March.

FAA (2010), *Commercial Space Transportation: 2009 Year in Review*, Federal Aviation Administration's Office of Commercial Space Transportation (FAA/AST), Washington, DC.

Fagerberg, J. (1996), "Technology and competitiveness", *Oxford Review of Economic Policy*, 12, 3, 39-51.

Indian Space Research Organisation (2010), *Annual Report 2009-2010*, ISRO, Bangalore.

INSEE (2008), *Impact du spatial sur l'économie de la Guyane*, Paris, September (in French).

INSEE (2010), *Les comptes économiques de la Guyane en 2009 : Le spatial préserve la croissance*, Paris, September (in French).

NASA (2010), *US Space Programme Spin-off*, Washington, DC. Available: *www.sti.nasa.gov/tto* [Accessed October].

Norwegian Space Centre (2010), *Norsk industri og-ESA deltakelse: Evaluering av industrielle ringvirkninger av Norsk deltakelse I ESAsamarbeidet*, Oslo, March (in Norwegian).

OECD (2008a), "Assessing the Socio-economic Impacts of Public R&D: Recent Practices and Perspectives", in OECD, *OECD Science, Technology and Industry Outlook 2008*, OECD Publishing, *http://dx.doi.org/10.1787/sti_outlook-2008-41-en*.

OECD (2008b), *Space Technologies and Climate Change: Implications for Water Management, Marine Resources and Maritime Transport*, OECD Publishing, *http://dx.doi.org/10.1787/9789264054196-en*.

OECD (2011), *The Space Economy at a Glance 2011*, OECD Publishing, *http://dx.doi.org/10.1787/9789264111790-en*.

Palmberg, C., H. Dernis and C. Miguet (2009), "Nanotechnology: An Overview Based on Indicators and Statistics", OECD Science, *Technology and Industry Working Papers*, No. 2009/07.

UK Space Agency (2010), *The Size and Health of the UK Space Industry*, Swindon, Wiltshire.

ANNEX A

Useful Manuals when Collecting/Reporting Data

Table A1.1. **Useful manuals when collecting/reporting data**

OECD Guide to Measuring the Information Society (2011)	This guide provides the statistical definitions, classifications and methods to measure and compare the information society across countries. It provides a standard reference for statisticians, analysts and policy-makers in the field. In particular, the guide should assist countries that want to start or develop new statistical programmes to measure the information society. Link: *www.oecd.org/sti/measuring-infoeconomy/guide*
OECD Patent Statistics Manual (2009)	The OECD Patent Statistics Manual provides guiding principles for the use of patent data in science and technology (S&T) measurement, and recommendations for the compilation and interpretation of patent indicators in this context. It aims to show what patent statistics can be used for, what they cannot be used for, and how to count patents in order to maximise information on S&T activities while minimising statistical noise and biases. Link: *www.oecd.org/document/29/0,3746,en_2649_34451_42168029_1_1_1_1,00.html*
Data and Metadata Reporting and Presentation Handbook (2007)	This manual provides a single comprehensive reference set of international guidelines and recommendations for the reporting and presentation of statistical data and metadata. Link: *www.oecd.org/dataoecd/46/17/37671574.pdf*
Eurostat-OECD Manual on Business Demography Statistics (2007)	This manual provides guidelines for the compilation of business demography indicators. Link: *www.oecd.org/dataoecd/8/8/39974460.pdf*
Oslo Manual: Guidelines for Collecting and Interpreting Innovation Data, 3rd Edition, OECD, Paris, OECD (2005),	The *Oslo Manual* is an international source of guidelines for the collection and use of data on innovation activities in industry. The third edition, released in 2005, is an update of the original 1992 and 1997 editions, taking account of the progress made in understanding the innovation process, the experience gained from the previous round of innovation surveys, the extension of the field of investigation to other sectors of industry and the latest revisions of international standard classifications. Link: *www.oecd.org/dataoecd/35/61/2367580.pdf*
Manual on Statistics of International Trade in Services (2002)	This manual is a joint publication of six agencies: the UN, EC, IMF, OECD, UNCTAD, and WTO. It sets out an internationally agreed framework for the compilation and reporting of statistics of international trade in services in a broad sense. Special emphasis is given to the statistical information needs of international trade negotiations and agreements. An update is expected by end-2010. Link: *www.oecd.org/dataoecd/32/45/2404428.pdf*
Frascati Manual: Proposed Standard Practice for Surveys on Research and Experimental Development (2002)	The *Frascati Manual* is the internationally recognized methodology for collecting and using R&D statistics. It includes definitions of basic concepts, data collection guidelines, and classifications for compiling statistics. This updated edition contains improved guidelines adjusted for changes in OECD economies, including measurement of service-sector R&D, R&D globalisation, and R&D human resources. Link: *www.oecd.org/document/6/0,3746,en_2649_34451_33828550_1_1_1_1,00.html*

ANNEX B

Glossary

Application for a patent: To obtain a patent, an application must be filed with the authorised body (Patent Office) with all the necessary documents and fees. The patent office will conduct an examination to decide whether to grant or reject the application.

Benefit transfer: A practice used to estimate economic values for ecosystem services by transferring information available from studies already completed in one location or context to another. This can be done as a unit value transfer or a function transfer.

Bibliometrics: Study of the quantitative data of the publication patterns of individual articles, journals, and books in order to analyse trends and make comparisons within a body of literature.

Costs avoidances: They are actual or imputed costs for preventing environmental deterioration by alternative production and consumption processes, or by the reduction of or abstention from economic activities. Costs can also be averted in times of natural and technological disasters by mitigation processes and systems, to which satellites contribute increasingly.

Gross Domestic Product (GDP): Gross domestic product is an aggregate measure of production equal to the sum of the gross values added of all resident institutional units engaged in production (plus any taxes, and minus any subsidies, on products not included in the value of their outputs). The sum of the final uses of goods and services (all uses except intermediate consumption) measured in purchasers' prices, less the value of imports of goods and services, or the sum of primary incomes distributed by resident producer units.

Gross Domestic Product (GDP) deflator: Volume of gross domestic product (GDP) calculated by recalculating the values of the various components of GDP at the constant prices of the previous year or of some fixed base year, frequently referred to as "GDP at constant prices", divided by GDP at current prices.

"Impacts indicators of the space economy": they include various types of socio-economic impacts derived from the development of space activities. Four main categories of impacts have been identified so far, although further work is certainly needed on the social dimensions of the use of space applications (*e.g.* reduction of the digital divide via satellite communications); they include: the creation of new commercial products and services, productivity/efficiency gains in diverse economic sectors (*e.g.* fisheries, airlines), economic growth regionally and nationally, and cost avoidances (*e.g.* floods).

International Patent Classification (IPC): The International Patent Classification, which is commonly referred to as the IPC, is based on an international multilateral treaty administered by WIPO. The IPC is an internationally recognised patent classification system, which provides a common classification for patents according to technology groups. IPC is periodically revised in order to improve the system and to take account of technical development. The current (eighth) edition of the IPC entered into force on 1 January 2006.

Intellectual property rights (IPR): IPR allows people to assert ownership rights on the outcomes of their creativity and innovative activity in the same way that they can own physical property. The four main types of intellectual property rights are: patents, trademarks, design and copyrights.

Input-output table: An input-output table is a means of presenting a detailed analysis of the process of production and the use of goods and services (products) and the income generated in that production.; they can be either in the form of *a)* supply and use tables or *b)* symmetric input-output tables.

Intensity indicators of the space economy: Intensity indicators are constituted by all the diverse outputs (products, services, science) that are produced or provided by the space sector. These outputs are very diverse in nature, from commercial revenues from industry, scientific productivity such as patents, to number of space missions or space launches.

Intermediate inputs/products: Goods and services, other than fixed assets, used as inputs into the production process of an establishment that are produced elsewhere in the economy or are imported. They may be either transformed or used up by the production process. Land, labour, and capital are primary inputs and are not included among intermediate inputs.

Intermediate inputs: Goods and services, other than fixed assets, used as inputs into the production process of an establishment that are produced elsewhere in the economy or are imported. They may be either transformed or used up by the production process. Land, labour, and capital are primary inputs and are not included among intermediate inputs. Also called: "intermediate products".

Market failure: General term describing situations in which market outcomes are not Pareto efficient. Market failures provide a rationale for government intervention. Context: There are a number of sources of market failure. For the purposes of competition policy, the most relevant of these is the existence of market power, or the absence of perfect competition. However, there are other types of market failure which may justify regulation or public ownership. When individuals or firms impose costs or benefits on others for which the market assigns no price, then an externality exists. Negative externalities arise when an individual or firm does not bear the costs of the harm it imposes (pollution, for example). Positive externalities arise when an individual or firm provides benefits for which it is not compensated. Finally, there are cases in which goods or services are not supplied by markets (or are supplied in insufficient quantities). This may arise because of the nature of the product, such as goods which have zero or low marginal costs and which it is difficult to exclude people from using (called public goods; for example, a lighthouse or national defence). It may also arise because of the nature of some markets, where risk is present (called incomplete markets; for example, certain types of medical insurance).

North American Industry Classification System (NAICS): An industry classification system used by statistical agencies to facilitate the collection, tabulation, presentation, and analysis of data relating to establishments. NAICS is erected on a production-oriented conceptual framework that groups establishments into industries according to similarity in the process used to produce goods or services. Under NAICS, an establishment is classified to one industry based on its primary activity. NAICS was developed jointly by Canada, Mexico, and the United States to provide comparability in economic statistics. It replaced the Standard Industrial Classification (SIC) system in 1997.

North American Product Classification System (NAPCS): A multi-phase effort by Canada, Mexico, and the United States to develop a comprehensive list of products, product definitions, and product codes that will be organized into an integrated demand-based classification framework that classifies both goods and services according to how they are principally used. It is intended that NAPCS will be used throughout the statistical community to co-ordinate the collection, tabulation, and analysis of data on the value of products produced by both goods- and services-producing industries and on the prices charged for those products. The focus in the initial phases of NAPCS will be directed at identifying and defining the products of services-producing industries. NAPCS will be a complementary but independent classification system to NAICS.

Output: Output consists of those goods or services that are produced within an establishment that become available for use outside that establishment, plus any goods and services produced for own final use. Such output may be:

- sold;
- entered into the producer's inventories prior to sale, barter, etc.;
- supplied to other establishments belonging to the same enterprise for use as intermediate inputs;
- retained by their owners for own final consumption or own gross fixed capital formation;
- supplied free, or sold at prices that are not economically significant to other institutional units;
- provided to their employees as compensation in kind or used for other payments in kind;
- bartered in exchange for other goods, services or assets.

Readiness indicators: The readiness factors include the different elements that are necessary for the development of space activities. These elements encompass the technical, financial and social infrastructures that enable the production of space-related hardware or the provision of services, *e.g.* indicators concerning the government budgets for space activities and human capital indicators.

Research and development (R&D): Research and experimental development (R&D) comprise creative work undertaken on a systematic basis in order to increase the stock of knowledge, including knowledge of man, culture and society, and the use of this stock of knowledge to devise new applications (*Frascati Manual*, 2002).

Small and medium-sized enterprises (SMEs): SMEs are non-subsidiary, independent firms which employ fewer than a given number of employees. This number varies across countries. The most frequent upper limit designating an SME is 250 employees, as in the European Union. However, some countries set the limit at 200 employees, while the United States considers SMEs to include firms with fewer than 500 employees. Small firms are generally those with fewer than 50 employees, while micro-enterprises have at most 10, or in some cases 5, workers. Financial assets are also used to define SMEs. In the European Union, a new definition came into force on 1 January 2005 applying to all Community acts and funding programmes as well as in the field of State aid where SMEs can be granted higher intensity of national and regional aid than large companies. The new definition provides for an increase in the financial ceilings: the turnover of medium-sized enterprises (50-249 employees) should not exceed EUR 50 million; that of small enterprises (10-49 employees) should not exceed EUR 10 million while that of micro firms (less than 10 employees) should not exceed EUR 2 million.

System of National Accounts (SNA) is the international standard for the compilation of national accounts statistics. It consists of a coherent, consistent and integrated set of macroeconomic accounts, balance sheets and tables based on a set of internationally agreed concepts, definitions, classifications and accounting rules. The System of National Accounts 1993 (SNA) has been prepared under the joint responsibility of the United Nations, the International Monetary Fund, the Commission of the European Communities, the OECD and the World Bank.

US Bureau of Economic Analysis (BEA): Part of the US Department of Commerce. The BEA's goal is to provide a clear picture of the United States economy by preparing, developing, and interpreting the national income and product accounts (summarized by the gross domestic product) as well as aggregate measures of international, regional, and state economic activity.

US Bureau of Labor Statistics (BLS): Part of the US Department of Labor. The BLS is the principal fact-finding agency for the federal government in the broad field of labor economics and statistics.

US Economic Census: The Economic Census (or census) is a periodic statistical program that obtains information about virtually every American establishment and publishes business statistics. In addition to regular statistical updates, the Bureau conducts a national census every five years. It provides information for calendar years ending in "2" and "7".

Sources: OECD (2002); OECD (2007); US Census Bureau (2008).

References

OECD (2002), *Frascati Manual: Proposed Standard Practice for Surveys on Research and Experimental Development*, The Measurement of Scientific and Technological Activities, OECD Publishing, *http://dx.doi.org/10.1787/9789264199040-en*.

OECD (2007), *OECD Glossary of Statistical Terms, webpage*, Paris, France. Available: *http://stats.oecd.org/glossary [Accessed 6 June 2007]*.

US Census Bureau (2008), *Glossary of Terms, webpage*, Washington, DC. Available: *http://bhs.econ.census.gov/BHS/glossary.html [Accessed 6 June 2008]*.

ANNEX C

Space Research and Development Appearing in Different Fields of Science and Technology

Table 7.A3.1. **Selection of categories based on 2007 revised version of the *Frascati Manual***

1. Natural Sciences	**1.2. Computer and information sciences** Computer sciences, information science and bioinformatics. **1.3. Physical sciences** Atomic, molecular and chemical physics (physics of atoms and molecules including collision, interaction with radiation; magnetic resonances; Moessbauer effect); Condensed matter physics (including formerly solid state physics, superconductivity); Particles and fields physics; Fluids and plasma physics (including surface physics); Optics (including laser optics and quantum optics), Acoustics; Astronomy (including astrophysics, space science). **1.4. Chemical sciences** Organic chemistry; Physical chemistry, Polymer science, Electrochemistry (dry cells, batteries, fuel cells, corrosion metals, electrolysis. **1.5. Earth and related environmental sciences** • Geosciences, multidisciplinary; Geochemistry and geophysics; Physical geography; Geology; Volcanology; Environmental sciences. • Astronomy (including astrophysics, space science)Aerospace engineering Mechanical engineering; Applied mechanics; Thermodynamics; Meteorology and atmospheric sciences; climatic research. • Oceanography, Hydrology, Water resources.
2. Engineering and Technology	**2.1. Civil engineering** Civil engineering; Architecture engineering; Construction engineering, Municipal and structural engineering; Transport engineering. **2.2. Electrical engineering, electronic engineering, information engineering** Electrical and electronic engineering; Robotics and automatic control; Automation and control systems; Communication engineering and systems; telecommunications; Computer hardware and architecture. **2.3. Mechanical engineering** • Mechanical engineering; Applied mechanics; Thermodynamics. • Aerospace engineering. • Nuclear related engineering. • Audio engineering, reliability analysis. **2.4. Chemical engineering** Chemical engineering (plants, products); Chemical process engineering. **2.5. Materials engineering** Materials engineering; Ceramics; Coating and films; Composites (including laminates, reinforced plastics, cermets, combined natural and synthetic fibre fabrics; filled composites); Paper and wood; textiles; including synthetic dyes, colours, fibres. **2.6. Medical engineering** Medical engineering; Medical laboratory technology (including laboratory samples analysis; diagnostic technologies). **2.7. Environmental engineering** Environmental and geological engineering, geotechnics; Petroleum engineering, (fuel, oils). Energy and fuels; Remote sensing; Mining and mineral processing; Marine engineering, sea vessels; Ocean engineering. **2.8. Environmental biotechnology** Environmental biotechnology; Bioremediation, diagnostic biotechnologies (DNA chips and biosensing devices) in environmental management; environmental biotechnology related ethics. **2.10. Nano-technology** • Nano-materials [production and properties]. • Nano-processes [applications on nano-scale].

Table 7.A3.1. **Selection of categories based on 2007 revised version of the *Frascati Manual*** (cont.)

3. Medical and Health Sciences	**3.3. Health sciences** • Health care sciences and services (including hospital administration, health care financing). • Public and environmental health; Tropical medicine; Parasitology; Infectious diseases; epidemiology. **3.4. Health biotechnology** Health-related biotechnology; Biomaterials (as related to medical implants, devices, sensors); Medical biotechnology related ethics.
4. Agricultural Sciences	**4.1. Agriculture, forestry, and fisheries** **4.2. Animal and dairy science** **4.4. Agricultural biotechnology** **4.5. Other agricultural sciences**

Source: Adapted from OECD (2007), *Revised Field of Science and Technology (FOS) Classification in the Frascati Manual*, Directorate for Science, Technology and Industry, Committee for Scientific and Technological Policy, Working Party of National Experts on Science and Technology Indicators, Paris.

ORGANISATION FOR ECONOMIC CO-OPERATION AND DEVELOPMENT

The OECD is a unique forum where governments work together to address the economic, social and environmental challenges of globalisation. The OECD is also at the forefront of efforts to understand and to help governments respond to new developments and concerns, such as corporate governance, the information economy and the challenges of an ageing population. The Organisation provides a setting where governments can compare policy experiences, seek answers to common problems, identify good practice and work to co-ordinate domestic and international policies.

The OECD member countries are: Australia, Austria, Belgium, Canada, Chile, the Czech Republic, Denmark, Estonia, Finland, France, Germany, Greece, Hungary, Iceland, Ireland, Israel, Italy, Japan, Korea, Luxembourg, Mexico, the Netherlands, New Zealand, Norway, Poland, Portugal, the Slovak Republic, Slovenia, Spain, Sweden, Switzerland, Turkey, the United Kingdom and the United States. The European Union takes part in the work of the OECD.

OECD Publishing disseminates widely the results of the Organisation's statistics gathering and research on economic, social and environmental issues, as well as the conventions, guidelines and standards agreed by its members.

OECD PUBLISHING, 2, rue André-Pascal, 75775 PARIS CEDEX 16
(92 2012 01 1 P) ISBN 978-92-64-12180-5 – No. 59875 2012

CPSIA information can be obtained
at www.ICGtesting.com
Printed in the USA
FSOW04n1403130417
33020FS

9 789264 121805